The First 30 Days

Off Alcohol & Drugs

12 low cost, low tech tips from the Old-timers of AA & NA with evidence-based results to support the newly recovering

Compiled by Shelly Marshall, BS CSAC
Editor: Gary Underwood, DDS

Digital ISBN 978-1-934569-28-3
Print ISBN 978-1-934569-55-9

Publisher
Day-By-Day.org

Table of Contents

Disclaimer iii
Affiliate Disclosure iv
Introduction vi

1 There is no magic but the first 30 days are crucial 1

2 Simple (often little understood) Solutions to the first
    30 days 12
    Presenting Problem ONE: Cravings for Substance of
        Choice & Depression 23
    Presenting Problem TWO: Denial 27
    Presenting Problem THREE: They don't trust you or the
        recovery process 33
    Presenting Problem FOUR: Desperation & Helplessness. 40
    Presenting Problem FIVE: Inability to focus, concentrate
        or retain information 52
    Presenting Problem SIX: Anger & Defiance 59
    Presenting Problem SEVEN: Self pity & Hopelessness ... 78
    Presenting Problem EIGHT: Fear, Panic, Dread 82
    Presenting Problem NINE: Nervousness, General Anxiety,
        Stress 89
    Presenting Problem TEN: Hopelessness or Alienation 93
    Presenting Problem ELEVEN: General feelings of nausea,
        sickness, deep muscle pain, stress, nervousness 100
    Presenting Problem TWELVE: Rough time sleeping
        and/or drowsiness even after full night's sleep 108

3 Final Thoughts 112

About Day By Day Recovery Resources 115
    World's Smallest Recovery Meditation Book (FREE) 115

Disclaimer

The information contained in this book, and our associated web sites and links, is provided as a service to the recovering community, and does not constitute medical advice. I try to provide quality information, but make no claims, promises or guarantees about the accuracy, completeness, or adequacy of the information contained in or linked in this ebook and its associated sites. As medical advice must be tailored to the specific circumstances and health of each individual, and medical knowledge is constantly changing, nothing provided herein should be used as a substitute for the advice, diagnosis, and treatment from your personal physician and addiction professional.

This manual does not provide medical advice nor is it intended to replace regular addiction treatment. The content of this manual including text, graphics, images, information obtained from web sites, and other material are intended for informational and educational purposes only. Always seek the advice of your physician or other qualified health care provider with any questions you may have regarding your medical condition. Never disregard professional medical advice or delay seeking it because of something you've read in this manual.

I am not a doctor. I am not even a Master's level clinician or clinical social worker. The alphabet soup behind my name stands for a Bachelors in Human Services and a Certification as a Substance Abuse Counselor. Some consider not having a doctorate to be an asset--I suppose it all depends on your perspective. I strongly support formal treatment and advocate for it when and where possible. However, I also respect the simple tried and true methods that work for alcoholics and addicts that were handed down from the Old Timers of Alcoholics Anonymous.

I began my own recovery in 1969 and have not found it necessary to take a drink or mind-affecting chemical since that time. I love the wisdom in the 12 Step programs and this book is intended to supplement what we already know about withdrawal from mind-affecting chemicals and beginning a life of recovery. Furthermore, my research in addictions has been published in several peer reviewed journals and I am confident in my ability to share the Old-timer's methods with you.

If you or a person you are working with have an addiction disorder and are experiencing a medical emergency, do not use this book to address it. I recommend going to your nearest emergency room.

If you do not agree to this disclaimer, please do not use the manual.

Affiliate Disclosure

I participate in a few affiliate programs, which means that if you purchase a product I've recommended through an affiliate link in this book, Day By Day[1] receives a small percentage of the purchase price, which helps to sustain our book donations to treatment centers via our *Pay It Forward* program.[2]

---

1 http://www.day-by-day.org/
2 https://www.pocketsponsor.com/payitforward.html

Introduction

Lets get honest. In early withdrawal from alcohol and other mind affecting chemicals, the newly clean and sober aren't likely to retain much. They make bad decisions (I think I'll take that job in Liberia), make no decisions (I should clean up the house before child protective services gets here but...), make grand decisions that don't make sense to anyone but them (moving to the Yukon will help my spirituality), and are otherwise generally messed up.

The old-timers in AA used to tell newcomers that they knew *nothing*—"Don't make a major decision during your first year; don't get married, divorced, quit a job, adopt a child from Botswana, decide to raise pit bulls, begin seeing a psychiatrist or quit seeing one," old timers repeated their wisdom over and over at meetings. Newcomers were told that their minds were not clear and their job was simple

    a) do not pick up,
    b) come to meetings and
    c) listen

Seasoned sponsors affirmed that the newly shaking drunk knew *nothing* about what the 12 Steps meant. Therefore, they did not have a program of their own, so were enjoined to work the program of their sponsor until such time as they built their own program.

Along with brutal honesty, old timers worked tirelessly with any newcomer who wanted to get off of alcohol and drugs. They opened their homes, wallets, and hearts to the common skid row drunk. Why did they do it? Well, the program from Alcoholic's Anonymous *says* to do it. In fact, it says if you *don't* work with newcomers, you are not going to stay sober!

Our very lives, as ex-problem drinkers, depend upon our constant thought of others and how we may help meet their needs. (P. 20 of Alcoholic's Anonymous [3])

Helping others is the foundation stone of your recovery. (P. 97 of Alcoholic's Anonymous)

But another more pragmatic reason why drunks worked so hard in the trenches with other drunks, is that nobody else wanted them! There wasn't big money in treating drunks back then. There were no treatment centers as we know them today —there were sanitariums, drunk tanks, missions on skid row, and if you had a drug problem? Forget it!

No one else wanted them!

So when one drunk began working with another as taught in AA, they had to aid in all aspects of the life of the person and family they helped, including getting them off mind-affecting chemicals—detoxing them. These lay people learned a lot of

---

3   https://amzn.to/2Kv9TnU

nifty tricks for stopping cravings, cramps, and sleeplessness, such as keeping a soda in your hand at all times to help with the habit of picking up a drink. (Today we would say "keep a mineral water in hand," but the sentiment is the same.) They told newcomers to drink honey in orange juice to stop the jitters and to suck on hard candies to counter the abrupt lack of alcoholic calories entering the body when detoxing. In fact, some meetings around the globe still offer little bowls of candy during meetings.

Factoid:[4] An estimated 88,000 people (approximately 62,000 men and 26,000 women) die from alcohol-related causes annually, making alcohol the third leading preventable cause of death in the United States. The first is tobacco, and the second is poor diet and physical inactivity.

Helping a newcomer stay sober was fraught with hazards. Newcomers, more often then not, went out again. They stole money from their benefactors, were often incredibly ungrateful, and could have created all kinds of havoc in the lives of those helping them. But at the same time, a lot of newcomers made it! They made it through the first 30 days, long enough to get clear and decide they wanted to continue in this new sober life.

And the art of one drunk caring for another or one druggie caring for another can not/should not be lost. This hands on, layman approach is incredibly precious and has a rich heritage in the anonymous programs. In this day and age of high tech, high cost treatment, the art of low cost, low tech support is retained and passed along in this little manual-- a manual with

---

4   https://www.niaaa.nih.gov/alcohol-health/overview-alcohol-consumption/alcohol-facts-and-statistics

tips to help others get through the first few months of staying clean and sober.

We only hope that you will share these tips with anyone that works with others in beginning recovery.

1 There is no magic but the first 30 days are crucial

We have no idea why one wins the recovery lottery

You do not have to be a licensed professional in order to help care for the person who wants to get clean and sober. You may be a sponsor from a 12 Step program, a volunteer in a halfway house, or a professional health care worker in a financially struggling treatment center. In any case, recovery from addiction to alcohol, meth, cocaine, opioids or any combination of chemicals is incredibly complicated and one treatment hat doesn't fit all. Even with the best treatment methods, some make it and many others don't. We have no idea why one person wins the recovery lottery and others die of the disease. What we do know is that no one begins recovery until they are off all mind-affecting chemicals. And that is where treatment and detox begin.

Treatment works best when viewed as a "gateway" into recovery from addiction to mind affecting chemicals. In fact, if treatment is available that is a *great* way to get started. But what if it isn't an option? Maybe your prospect doesn't have much money and doesn't qualify for subsidized care. What if the person you want to help has gone through multiple centers and never got it—but you think this time, they might be serious. What if they *refuse* treatment because of their job or religion but you think they have a chance and offer to help? Maybe treatment is an option but the center you are considering is struggling with financial issues. You want to do as much as you can for your clients or sponsees but you must consider the cost.

Believe it or not, there are solutions that work great and cost practically nothing. Sometimes you may use all the solutions we suggest in this little manual, or you may pick and choose depending on the situation. You don't have to have a lot of money, a cracker jack treatment center, or an alphabet soup array behind your name in order to help. Simple and practical solutions are available and in many cases are *more* effective than their high tech, high cost counter parts.

Stretch that recovery dollar.

Factoid[5] The highest death rate due to excessive drinking was in New Mexico (51 deaths per 100,000 population), and the lowest was in New Jersey (19.1 per 100,000).

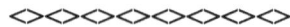

Depending on your unique situation and the person(s) you want to help, we explore 12 strategies that may be incorporated into a care plan and/or sponsorship approach that really help beginners in recovery.

SIMPLE APPROACHES FOR 30 TO 90 DAYS

People in their first 30 to 90 days off alcohol and other drugs are out of their minds. They are confused, have a short attention span, and often make irrational decisions, have unrealistic expectations, experience paranoia, and they think they are "just fine."

What works best in the first three months off mind affecting chemicals (either legal or illegal substances), are simple approaches. The more basic, the better. The Old Timers were chock full of tid-bits of information that helped their prospects stay clean and sober. If you are in Alcoholic's Anonymous—many of the Old Timers from the 50s and 60s are still around and still dispensing advice (they would say *"suggestions,"* not advice) about helping a person lay off booze. Most of what they suggest will also apply to helping a person lay off other drugs, as well.

NOT JUST FOR 12 STEP MEMBERS

Although many of the suggestions in this manual are based on

---

5 http://www.cdc.gov/media/releases/2014/p0626-excessive-drinking.html

the experiences of the those who started AA, a few are newer approaches from evidence-based best practices. Do not think this is just a manual for those in 12 Step programs. It is for *anyone* who wants to help another who is trying to get off drugs and alcohol. The basis for these suggestions, for the most part, come from people in 12 Step programs but much of the information is also drawn from medical and psychological research. This is NOT a manual to get people sober as in the 12 Steps or Narkanon—it is not a program to maintain sobriety[6]—it is for the scrambled body and mind of the person trying to get off alcohol and other drugs, without using drugs and high tech expensive approaches.

THIS IS A BASIC PRIMER

We'll leave the social, mental, and spiritual support to Alcoholic's Anonymous, Narcotics Anonymous, Chemically Dependent Anonymous, addiction professionals, and religious workers who tackle such things. This is a very BASIC PRIMER for treatment center personnel, the sponsor or caretaker, the ones who want to help the newcomer stop craving, get some sleep, stop shaking, calm down, clear the head, and get motivated.

Looking for prospects to help

So if you want to help your prospect prepare them-self to hear the message of recovery and they are not in formal treatment for whatever reason, then this is the manual for you.

---
6   http://www.drugabuse.gov/frequently-asked-questions#detox

INITIAL WITHDRAWAL IS DANGEROUS

Despite advances in medications to reduce cravings and ease withdrawal symptoms, prescriptions such as Naltrexone, Acamprosate, Subutex and Suboxone (approved by the FDA for this purpose) or off label medications like Topiramate, Rimonabant, Clonidine, ondarnstron (Zofran) sertraline (Zoloft), which are wonderful at times, there is no magic in getting off drugs and staying clean and sober. It takes hard work, great support, sometimes continuing therapy, and a vigilance unknown to those who don't suffer from a chronic disease.

Before you begin the simple solutions outlined in this manual, understand that initial withdrawal from alcohol and other drugs is physically very serious. Because of that, even if your prospect is not going into formal treatment, they must use some form of assisted withdrawal. This can be a brief detox clinic lasting five days or less. Often a more popular "home assisted" withdrawal is available where professionals allow a person to stay home but monitor them frequently as they physically withdraw. This is usually done within seven days.

The first week is dangerous, depending on the drug(s) and severity of dependence. (*Different drugs react differently with body chemistry so it is difficult to be more specific—but the professionals can assess your prospect and let you know.*) The first week is normally when the body reacts most violently to being deprived of its drug of choice from convulsions to choking on their own vomit; you do not want to be the one responsible for the initial detox. So insist that your prospect use professional oversight and you become the support person —or feet on the ground so to speak. The professional may prescribe medications to help—again this depends on what they are addicted to and how severe the physical dependence. You do not make that choice, but allow the professionals to make it and you assist the professionals. As the person you are helping goes through their first week, you read, review, and prepare for the weeks and months ahead with this manual.

Where do you find the "assisted detox" professionals? You can ask members of 12 Step programs, especially if they also work as a professional in the field. You can look them up online by searching for "home assisted detox" or "medically assisted detox." Often local church groups may know. And the best place to begin is with your prospect's health care professional: family doctor or physician's assistant. Old Timers in 12 Step groups often bypassed the professionals when helping a newcomer; basically they didn't have a choice. Today, we do. The field of substance dependence has grown exponentially and even if your helpee will not/can not use a treatment center per se and they let you help, you must insist they be monitored by medical professionals during the first week.

JONESING FOR THOSE DARN DRUGS

"I know you want a drink. Just don't pick up the first one."

After the crucial physical detox, the hardest part for the alcoholic and addict in recovery is getting past the first 30 to 90 days while shaking their hunger for drugs. This is where *you* come in. Many well meaning family members or even professionals will throw newcomers into complicated approaches that do nothing but baffle their muddled alcoholic minds. In fact, family, group, and couples counseling or other psychotherapies in the first few months may be counter-productive[7] to someone coming off drugs who can barely put two thoughts together. Your job is to keep them focused on not picking up and using the simple solutions in this manual, not solving life-long problems.

In the first 30 days many treatment centers tackle too much too soon. The professionals know how many issues need to be addressed for long term recovery and, bless them, they try to do it. Yet we know that the mind of the addict is so screwed up initially—the patient will hardly remember a thing covered in treatment. Serious problems with the physical body have to be managed first. The mind, emotions, and spirit come later. The body desperately attempts to shake off the poisons and damage and regain neuro-chemical balance. Of course we tweak the mind and spirit when we can, but in the first 30 days, caretakers must be realistic about what their prospects can and cannot absorb, understand or retain.

Overview of the problems treatment addresses

This is a description of what goes on with patients admitted to a treatment center.

Physical:

Cravings for substance of choice, nervousness, sleeplessness, inability to focus, twitchiness, general feelings of nausea and sickness, shaking limbs, trembling, deep muscle pain

---

7 http://psychcentral.com/disorders/sx16t.htm

Mental:

Anger and defiance, denial, obsessions, distrust of you and recovery, short attention spans, anxiousness, confusion, self-pity, depression, ambivalence

Spiritual:

Fear and panic, dread, desperation, helplessness, hopelessness, alienation, abandonment

There is no requirement for people to feel miserable when coming off drugs.

We hear all the time about this new therapy and that new therapy for addiction. Then independent research is done (as opposed to in-house research) and we find that folks who go to AA do better than those that don't (Vaillant January 2003[8] and

---

8   http://onlinelibrary.wiley.com/doi/10.1046/j.1360-0443.2003.00422.x/abstract

in the Journal for Psychoactive Drugs 2010)[9]. We wonder if our centers are effective. We have found that most people who go through treatment don't stay sober thereafter no matter what method or medicines the center uses. So the question naturally arises—should we even send people to treatment in the first place if recovery rates are so low? Bearing in mind that no matter how low some of the cancer cure rates are, we would not dream of *not treating* its victims. Here is what we do know about addiction recovery:

1. You don't need AA, NA or any 12 Step program to recover
2. You don't need treatment to recover from addiction
3. People who do both are more likely to maintain abstinence[10] than people who do either alone

Factoid:[11] *{Professionals have} known for quite some time that it takes about 5 years for the average addict to achieve self-sustainable recovery - i.e., ability to maintain recovery without extraordinary intervention or structured support. Despite this knowledge, the bulk of NIDA research has focused on understanding the mechanisms of addiction with the main thrust being in the direction of enhanced treatments. The problem persists that treatments are short-term, and recovery is long-term.*

DON'T GO CRAZY CRAMMING EVERY METHOD INTO THE FIRST 30 DAYS

---

9   https://www.ncbi.nlm.nih.gov/pmc/articles/PMC3057870/
10 http://www.scientificamerican.com/article/does-alcoholics-anonymous-work/
11 https://tinyurl.com/y5qll6uo

Since the 30s when AA proved that alcoholics are not hopeless and professionals took up the cause of recovery, experts have gone crazy trying to cram all this good stuff we've learned into 30 short and terrifying days of treatment. Remember the saying about the 60s? If you remember the 60s, you weren't there. Something similar could be said about recovery—if you remember what you learned in the first 30 days, you probably do not suffer from alcoholism.

What newly sober alcoholic or addict can string two coherent thoughts together, much less remember all the bio, social, psycho lessons taught in treatment?At best, treatment will point the patient in the right direction, at worse it will make things more complicated. Many centers have stated they need patients for ninety days or six months or even a year. And to address the issues inherent in the disease, *they are right.* BUT who has that kind of money? Or time? Or jobs that will allow extended care leaves? Certainly public health care won't cover extended treatment. Extended treatment for all the addicts and alcoholics who need it is not sustainable. Professionals are lucky in most instances to get the traditional 30 day treatment program approved by payers. Detox is usually a few days and wham, they're out on the streets again.

Even if your prospect has the money or insurance to cover it, in 30 days the problems of inner child issues, sexual abuse, rebuilding a self-image, origins of addiction, learning new social skills, dealing with the familial issues, *cannot be solved*! Even if they could, that would not help alcoholics stay away from alcohol and drugs!
Initial treatment can realistically do only these things
    Detoxify the body, safely
    Encourage rudimentary motivation,
    Act as a conduit into some program/institution that will help maintain abstinence for the rest of their life.

HAVE YOU THE DEDICATION TO HELP?

So if the experts can't do all that much initially, what can you the treatment provider, you the caretaker/family member, or you the sponsor or sober coach do to really *really* help your newcomer through the first 30 days?

You have the time, interest, and commitment to help. You may work in a treatment center or half way house without access to high cost-high tech approaches to treatment—whose initial effectiveness may be dubious in any case. You may be a family member or a sponsor to a newcomer who can't get into treatment or won't go to treatment; so what can you do?

You take the advice of the Old-timers, mix in a little research across several disciplines. and use some common sense. Here are 12 simple (often little understood) solutions for the first 30 days.

2 Simple (often little understood) Solutions to the first 30 days

The fact that someone coming off mind-affecting chemicals fights an ungodly compulsion for the very thing they know is killing them, is understood by us in the profession. When the cravings are not satisfied, patients plummet into depression. Unfortunately, a lot of professionals try to treat the depression as a separate phenomenon, when depression usually is a side affect of not getting the drug their body is so used to.

There are new drugs

There are new drugs that purportedly help with these symptoms of withdrawal: naltrexone, acomprosate, ondarnstron (Sofranm) sertraline (Zoloft)—some claim these prescriptions work great and some say not so much. Old

Timers in AA suggested drinking orange juice with honey in it and to eat candy! Some had newcomers take B vitamins for the nerves.

In the early 70's, a group of drunks ran a halfway house in Denver Colorado called "the Hand of Hope." It was actually for those who had drug addictions along with their alcoholism and were trying to get help but no treatment centers would take them on. So they came to the Hand of Hope to get clean and sober. A professional, Dr. Larry from Saint Luke's in Denver—who ran their alcoholism ward, volunteered to help the group of drunks help the addicts. He suggested they give the detoxing person calcium and magnesium for cramps, convulsions, and insomnia. The housefather bought big bottles of calcium and magnesium which were handed out like candy. The guys did sleep better, the DT's lasted less time, and no one died at the Hand of Hope. This is not to say that you should treat someone going through withdrawal in your basement like they did at the Hand of Hope—*it is very dangerous* and withdrawal should be treated at a detox center. But once they leave detoxification, ask their medical professional if taking calcium and magnesium might not be a good idea.

Coffee is a natural anti-depressant.

Still today, many treatment centers adhere to nutritional guidelines to counter cravings and depression. They often don't allow sugary drinks, high calorie snacks, caffeinated beverages, etc. And all indications demonstrate that good nutrition does help with withdrawal[12] and getting addicts back on their feet in short order.

Although, some would disagree, I don't think it helps to cut out coffee and tea during withdrawal. In fact studies show caffeine helps alertness (about 3 cups a day) and fights depression as demonstrated in this YouTube report[13] covering a study in the *Journal of the American Medical Association*.[14] Coffee actually is a natural antidepressant and good for you in numerous ways we didn't understand before, see *Johns Hopkins University School of Medicine,* 9 Reasons Why (the Right Amount of) Coffee Is Good for You.)[15] and in the New York times article in January 26, 2010 they ran an article extolling the many health benefits of coffee "Coffee as a Health Drink? Studies Find Some Benefits.[16]" I suspect that the Old Timers in AA would never suggest to cut out coffee during withdrawal (provided of course your prospect doesn't have a condition that precludes using caffeinated beverages like diabetes, arrhythmias, or high blood pressure).

Besides providing 3 healthy meals daily, here are some loose guidelines in nutrition if you are helping someone in their first 30 days:

1. Don't allow sugary (sugar added) drinks (or those that add chemical sweeteners)

2. Do allow 100% juices and orange juice with honey (as was passed down from the Old-timers—but not if their physical condition such as diabetes precludes it--then consider a stevia[17] or monk fruit product)

3. For the first year, keep a drink in their hand at the times they would normally drink alcohol to help with the

---

12 http://alcoholicsvictorious.org/faq/diet
13 https://www.youtube.com/watch?v=Uytn9-QdSkA
14 https://tinyurl.com/y4c6a2hz
15 https://tinyurl.com/y3slqs4b
16 http://www.nytimes.com/2006/08/15/health/nutrition/15coff.html?_r=0
17 http://www.livescience.com/39601-stevia-facts-safety.html

habitual part of learning not to drink—use coffee or a mineral water instead.

4. Offer coffee and tea with honey for those who want it and don't have health issues that preclude it.

5. Have them snack on walnuts, pine nuts and almonds (which are high in minerals, protein, and give good nutritive-dense energy)

Ask their health care professional about increasing supplements during the first few months—giving potassium, calcium and magnesium, B 12 shots, B complex, Folic Acid and C.

HOME-BASED DETOXIFICATION VERSES CLINICAL DETOXIFICATION

> **Warning** (at the risk of boring you, we once again warn): "Detoxification" the word used by health care professionals and "Drying out" words used by the layman, is nothing to take lightly. This manual is not suggesting you go it alone with your prospect. During this initial phase of helping the newcomer, you need supervision because they may need to use medicine that is only available by prescription. In addition, you are not qualified to know what symptoms constitute a medical emergency.

> **Factoid**:[18] *Withdrawal seizures are more common in patients who have a history of multiple episodes of detoxification.*

Even though the person you want to help *begs* you to help them and not seek the advice of professionals—once again we

---
18 http://www.aafp.org/afp/2004/0315/p1443.html#

caution, insist on a professional evaluation. It is the responsibility of the health care professional and the person you want to help to make the decision if they want to do a home-based or a clinical detoxification during the first week or so. It is not your decision. So even if they choose to withdraw at home with your help, keep some emergency numbers handy, like their regular doctor's off hours number, the local addiction service number, and the local ambulance.

They may experience paranoia during withdrawal

If you know from experience that your prospect tends to suffer from severe withdrawal symptoms, such as vomiting, dehydration, tremors, or even hallucinations and paranoia, you should insist they detox in a supervised setting such as a hospital or clinic.

On the other hand, the family physician or your health clinic may want to do a home-assisted withdrawal and your help to monitor them will be invaluable. Most people[19] (over 90%) can successfully withdrawal on their own. "Successfully" meaning they probably won't die from withdrawal. The real success will be if you can help them abstain—not return to their drug of choice.

Factoid:[20] *According to a NIDA-funded clinical trial. Researchers Dr. Eric Collins and colleagues at the College of Physicians and Surgeons of Columbia University concluded that ultrarapid detox techniques don't make withdrawal easier. The new findings corroborate those of three international studies.*

THE CRUCIAL FIRST WEEK

Whichever method of withdrawal your helpee chooses, the first three days are of course usually the worst, depending on the drug they are withdrawing from. Although every body and its chemistry is different, most of the physical symptoms of withdrawal from mind affecting-physically addicting chemicals will only last from one to two weeks.

Here is an idea of what you may be dealing with depending on which drug they most used in their active addiction, opiates, depressives including alcohol, and stimulants including :

OPIATES: including illegal drugs like heroin, legal like methadone, and prescription pain medications such as Codeine, Duragesic (fentanyl), and Oxycodone. Withdrawal from opiates can be horrendously painful, but usually not life threatening. About 9% of the population is believed to misuse

---
19 http://www.aafp.org/afp/2004/0315/p1443.html#
20 https://archives.drugabuse.gov/news-events/nida-notes/2006/10/study-finds-withdrawal-no-easier-ultrarapid-opiate-detox

opiates over the course of their lifetime

Early symptoms of withdrawal from opiates include:
Runny eyes and nose
Agitation and nervousness
Sleeplessness and yawning
Sweating

Later withdrawal symptoms from opiates include
Cramping
Cravings
Diarrhea
Skin crawling
Dilated pupils
Sick to the stomach (burning in stomach)
No appetite
Vomiting
Insomnia

Factoid:[21] *Every day, more than 130 people in the United States die after overdosing on opioids. The misuse of and addiction to opioids—including prescription pain relievers, heroin, and synthetic opioids such as fentanyl—is a serious national crisis that affects public health as well as social and economic welfare. Prescription opioid misuse alone costs the United States a whopping $78.5 billion a year, including the costs of healthcare, lost productivity, addiction treatment, and criminal justice involvement.*

DEPRESSANTS: *including alcohol, and tranquilizers like Valium, Seroquel, Haldol, Xanax, Klonopin, Halcion and*

---
21 https://www.drugabuse.gov/drugs-abuse/opioids/opioid-overdose-crisis

Librium. Alcohol withdrawal begins about 8 hours after the last drink, but for periodics, withdrawal can start days later. Symptoms usually peak within 72 hours, but may persist for weeks. The rest of the depressants usually have similar withdrawal patterns but may lag a day or so in the onset of symptoms.

Early symptoms of withdrawal from Alcohol and other depressants:
    Anxiety or nervousness
    Depression
    Emotional volatility
    Jitters and shaky hands

Later symptoms of withdrawal from Alcohol and other depressants:
    Bad dreams
    Fuzzy thinking
    Cravings
    Clammy skin and sweating
    Enlarged (dilated) pupils
    Headache
    Insomnia
    Loss of appetite and weight loss
    Nausea and vomiting
    Rapid heart rate

Loss of appetite and weight loss is one of many withdrawal symptoms

Symptoms from a severe withdrawal called delirium tremens:
Fever
Hallucinations
Seizures
Severe confusion

Factoid:[22] *Benzodiazepines were developed to replace barbiturates, though they still share many of the undesirable side effects. Some examples are Valium®, Xanax®, Halcion®, Ativan®, Klonopin® and Restoril®.*

STIMULANTS: *including prescription stimulants, such as Adderall, Concerta, and Ritalin street drugs such as cocaine, crack, amphetamines, and methamphetamines.* Stimulant withdrawal is probably not life-threatening, but extreme emotional reactions and agitation will be present. Withdrawal time is based on the amount and frequency of stimulants they used. The worst symptoms last from 3 to 5 days from last use, but triggers can bring on cravings years after they have quit.

Early symptoms of withdrawal from Stimulants:
Loss of appetite
Tired
Confusion
Fears
Restlessness, depression, and unease
Speedy-buzzy feeling throughout body, "crashing"

Later symptoms of withdrawal from Stimulants:
Intense and unpleasant dreams

---
22 https://www.dea.gov/taxonomy/term/316

Disinterest in surroundings
Increased appetite
Inability to think straight
Cravings

Factoid[23]: *The use of cocaine for recreational purposes has been reported to induce signs of cocaine induced psychosis. In addition to greater amounts of anger and violence tendencies, they are subject to symptoms of delirium which can include "severe blood pressure changes," fluctuation in pulse, and extreme sweating. The individual may become extremely paranoid and refuse to believe what you and others say, making it difficult to help them.*

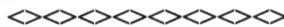

OTC HELP

Most of the time these symptoms can be managed with over the counter medications like pain killers, diarrhea medicine, digestion aids, and common teas. But remember that the one you are helping may have conditions where some OTCs would be contraindicated—such as sweetened preparations for diabetics or NSAIDs for someone on a blood thinner. This is another reason to consult and use a medical professional while trying to help someone—you don't want to make what seems like a harmless recommendation and have it seriously endanger your prospect.

There are many online suggestions and plans for withdrawing from various drugs such as the Thomas Recipe for Withdrawal from Opiates. You can google these layman detox suggestions but again we will caution you to only take the suggestions

---

23 https://www.disorders.org/cocaine-addiction/signs-and-symptoms-of-cocaine-induced-psychosis/

under the supervision of a medical professional who understands detoxification from mind-affecting, mood altering drugs. Nutritional supplements and OTCs can be very useful *and also dangerous* if you don't have all the information you need.

Besides the emotional support your presence provides and feeding your newcomer foods their bodies need to heal safely, here are 12 PRESENTING PROBLEMS handed down from the old timers in recovery that have low-tech low-cost solutions you may want to use.

Presenting Problem ONE: Cravings for Substance of Choice & Depression

Boy, this is the killer. The person you are helping knows they need to get off drugs, but getting that first fix, pill or drink is all they think about. They are not stupid. You might even think they are not motivated--but I have seen some of the most motivated people in the world still not be able to resist craving. In order to get past this hump, the situation has to get so bad that the pain of using is *worse* than the pain of not using..some never reach that threshold.

A few drugs are so intense that in controlled experiments scientists found that rats "would cross a highly electrified floor to receive the stimulation–a floor that even rats starved for 24 hours would not cross for food.[24]" Cravings are stronger than non-addicted people understand. But that doesn't mean we are helpless at the gates of brain chemistry. There are measures we can take.

TRY THIS: Feed your prospect a potato 30 minutes before bed!

No kidding. The spud solution helps. What does it do? Research from the University of Pittsburgh and from MIT have looked at the diet to help the body raise serotonin levels. Raising serotonin levels is the way many mood enhancing drugs work making you feel more confident, competent, creative and optimistic. But rather than taking a prescription with side affects, that may cost boo koo bucks, and needs a physician to prescribe—why not try nutrition first? And, it seems the lowly potato can raise serotonin in your brain.

---

24 http://alfre.dk/the-pleasure-center/

Factoid:[25] *The potato belongs to the Solanaceae or nightshade family whose other members include tomatoes, eggplants, peppers, and tomatillos. They are the swollen portion of the underground stem which is called a tuber and is designed to provide food for the green leafy portion of the plant. If allowed to flower and fruit, the potato plant will bear an inedible fruit resembling a tomato.*

Big results from a single nightly spud 30 minutes before bed.

Have the newcomer eat their potato baked, mashed, roasted, cut into oven fries or grated into hash browns. Just be sure they *eat the skin*. This raises tryptophan from the blood into the brain. Why do we care about that? The body uses tryptophan to make serotonin. And we have learned that serotonin is the brain chemical that makes us feel mellow and happy, as well as being a sleep aid.

---

25 http://www.whfoods.com/genpage.php?tname=foodspice&dbid=48

In the context of withdrawal it may help our patient to "just say no" to the drug of choice by putting the brakes on their impulsively.

Discussion on the role of diet in raising serotonin levels were initiated in the research of Madelyn Fernstrom, Ph.D at the University of Pittsburgh and Wurtman and Wurtman at MIT[26] *(Brain Serotonin, Carbohydrate-craving, obesity and depression. Adv Exp Med Biol, 1996. 398: p. 35-41)*

In addition, neurochemical studies show that chronic alcoholics have lower levels of serotonin in the brain. Serotonin levels fall during alcohol withdrawal and remain low for more than 2 weeks, which can explain anxiety, panic, sleeplessness and other symptoms during withdrawal From PubMed: Carbohydrate craving by alcohol-dependent men during sobriety: relationship to nutrition and serotonergic function.[27]

For a lot of research references read Kathleen DesMaisons, specialist in Addictive Nutrition and author of the book "Potatoes Not Prozac.[28]" This book (and her website) have pages of research to bolster her claim that raising serotonin in the brain helps with addiction recovery. Although I don't usually tout one product over another, Ms. DesMaison's work is very helpful here.

RECAP

To help with cravings and depression:[29] Try serving a potato 30 minutes before bed. It can be baked, mashed, roasted, cut into oven fries or grated into hash browns—but it must contain

---

26 http://www.ncbi.nlm.nih.gov/pubmed/8697046
27 https://www.ncbi.nlm.nih.gov/pubmed/10832904
28 https://amzn.to/2JSRthW
29 http://www.radiantrecovery.com/4r.htm

the skin. You may top it with anything you like *except* foods that contain a protein. Protein eaten along with the potato at bedtime will interfere with the serotonin-making process. Good toppings are butter, margarine, salsa, mustard, spices, olive oil or flaxseed oil. Toppings you should NOT use are cheese, sour cream, bacon bits, or cream of chicken soup. (excerpted from RadiantRecovery.com)

Presenting Problem TWO: Denial

"Not me, I'm different; you don't understand," ah, the war cry of the addicted,"I'm different..." therefore anything anyone suggests doesn't apply to them! So your battle with someone you want to help is getting past the excuses of why none of this applies to them, also known as *denial*. It takes many forms, even *after* they admit they have a problem and say, " my addiction is no one else's business because I'm not hurting anyone but myself."

Example. When trying to help:

You suggest they don't go to the drug store unaccompanied for a few months--because the temptation to buy cough syrup or grab a bottle is too great.

> Denial, "I am not *that* weak. I only need to stop in and get a soda after work. I won't even walk past the cough syrup." *Your helpee uses in less than a week.*

You tell your prospect that their family and friends suffer from their drinking.

> Denial, "I know I'm an alcoholic but I'm not hurting anybody so leave me alone."

I'm not hurting anyone but myself

You suggest that they have a serious drinking problem.

Denial, "All my friends and most of my family drink too. I've only had one DUI because the cop set an entrapment down the road from the bar..."

Factoid:[30] *Even with abject proof of an events occurrence, someone in denial is highly unlikely to fully accept the particular reality that their mind has decided they cannot cope with. They are more likely in that instance to use projection or minimization or to continue or revert back to being in full blown denial.*

Denial is like that. Whatever you say, your prospect counters it with a doozie of an excuse. They are so very creative.

I once worked at Denver General as an intern on the Detoxification unit. They had a group of revolving skid row winos who wanted nothing to do with sobriety. Most of them lived on the streets, were brought in by police or AA folk and usually were on the verge of death before being dumped off at the emergency room doors. Invariably, you would talk to them and they explained why they were not alcoholic (a dirty word) and were just down on their luck, lost a job, got out of the service and just hadn't got it together yet—not a one of them would say it was the hooch that was bringing them down.

The hospital staff were desperate to get them to go to AA meetings or at the very least admit they were a wino—just admit it!

So I considered the problem at Denver General. These guys did not identify as alkies. What would it take to give them

---

30 http://www.urbandictionary.com/define.php?term=Denial

some insight? At speakers meetings in 12 Step programs, when a speaker is particularly good, the whole audience can be put to spasms of belly laughs at the most grotesque drunk-a-logs. People who think that puking on yourself and lying in your own urine is gross, can suddenly laugh about it and remember when it happened to them. The worst circumstances turn into an admittable occurrence. The thing they did not want to see can now be seen through laughter—if we can't see ourselves through shame, we can at least glimpse through the eyes of mirth.

So I gathered up a stack of tapes (yes we were still into cassettes in those days), and started group therapy which consisted of listening to the drunk-a-logs of some of the funniest speakers in AA history. The Denver detox winos loved it, to say the least. We listened to the speakers and then shared in group. That was it. Beaten and scowling, gruff and ashamed, these guys responded and responded in a big way.

The rest of the staff could not believe the way these men (and some women) began to open up. They talked, shared, laughed, and bragged... and we made progress. No, not all of them ran to join a 12 Step group. But a handful did. And a handful was more than had ever happened before.

Laughter allows people to see themselves.

You see, not only did laughter allow these guys to see themselves and identify, it made AA not such a scary fellowship after all. It gave them permission to be a drunk and then to seek the companionship of other drunks. It opened a door. An important one. So when you are working with denial in your prospect, Infotainment is one of the best and fastest ways to help open the doors for them. (*Hollywood in the classroom: using feature films to teach. Nurse Educ.*[31] *2005 may-June;30(3):113-6 Masters JC*)

TRY THIS: Infotainment

1. *Humorous talks from the 12 Step Fellowships (try Youtube and Speaker Tape download sites)*

Some examples from Youtube:
Mickey B. AA Speaker "His Funniest talk EVER!"
//www.youtube.com/watch?v=MJXNmvDvXn4
Clancy I. - AA Speaker - One of his funniest talks ever!
//www.youtube.com/watch?v=hoxofrHTIwE
Scott R. - AA Speaker - "We are not a glum lot!" (Very funny!)
//www.youtube.com/watch?v=wRgnmnOi0k8
Karin B. - NA Speaker - "An Inspiration for Us All" - Drug Addiction Recovery
//www.youtube.com/watch?v=BAHgzt7neck
Layla N. CA speaker sharing on cocaine addiction recovery at a CA meeting
//www.youtube.com/watch?v=0tySJ4Qbg64

Speaker Tape Sites for free download:
Recovery Is Good For You
//www.elmoware.com/
12 Step Pod Casts from iTune
//itunes.apple.com/us/podcast/12-step-podcast/id152218998?mt=2
NA Carry the Message of Recovery
//carrythemessage.com/

---

31 http://www.ncbi.nlm.nih.gov/pubmed/15900204

2. Cinamatherpay: Movies they can identify with (try Amazon, Netflicks or Hulu.com)

28 Days //amzn.to/2MpObo8
The Anonymous People
A Woman Under the Influence //amzn.to/2IkaxlI
Affliction //amzn.to/2IioXD5
Barfly //amzn.to/2QHbKrm
Blow //amzn.to/2WhrZkU
Burnt //amzn.to/2JUroyK
Half Baked //amzn.to/2MoywWn
Clean and Sober //amzn.to/2MnyFJB
Flight //amzn.to/2WE6cTS
Traffic //amzn.to/2ELt5u7
Leaving Las Vegas //amzn.to/2WitJu1
Fear and Loathing in Las Vegas //amzn.to/2WF1lSa
Pay it Forward //amzn.to/2ERSS4a
Crazy Heart //amzn.to/2ER8gO5
Everything Must Go //amzn.to/2WHOAq1
Half Nelson //amzn.to/2Ii5UZq
The Fighter //amzn.to/2IcX5jN
Silver Linings Playbook //amzn.to/2WmTBoL
Stewart Saves His Family //amzn.to/2WhatNz
The Basketball Diaries //amzn.to/2ENpn3a
Home Run //amzn.to/2QKIJek
When a Man Loves a Woman //amzn.to/2WkpA8R
Thanks for Sharing //amzn.to/2JYIhZt

Some hints: Although laughter is usually the fastest way to break through denial, other poignant films can be helpful too. If your prospect doesn't want to listen, then offer them an enticement such as, "Hey listen to this with me, its only 45 minutes, and then I'll watch Star Trek with you."

Keep in mind, links change frequently. I try to keep up, but if any of the links are broken, simply search the net for substitutes—you may find much better Recovery Infotainment than I found here, anyway.

RECAP

Author Mark Worden has a great article on denial that pretty much defines the problem with the alcoholic and addict. His article, "I'm No Alcoholic" says a person recovers from denial in three stages: Recognition, Acceptance, and Surrender. The very best way we have found to get a person through these stages is by getting them to *see* themselves--not an easy task. After all, who wants to see the mess they themselves created? But through the eyes of mirth, the person suffering just might get a glimpse of themselves. Laughter and infotainment are like fast tracks through the three stages of Recognition, Acceptance, and Surrender.

Deja brew: The feeling that you've had this hangover before.

Presenting Problem THREE: They don't trust you or the recovery process

Many people who live with and work with the addicted ask, "How do you trust an alcoholic?" or "How do you trust a junkie?" We know you don't (initially). We may not find it easy or justified to trust the newly recovering and that is prudent. Conversely, the addicted have issues of their own and ask themselves, "How do you trust treatment centers, law enforcement, family who desert you, and friends who talk behind your back?" It is an understatement to say that people in recovery have trust issues of their own.

TRY THIS: Get pets to build the trust

Pet facilitated recovery works when many other things don't. When contemplating helping others, we usually think of doctors, nurses, counselors, and visiting angels—but how often do we think of dogs and cats and horses? Yet it seems that animals may be able to help open up alcoholics and addicts long before a professional breaks through.

Animals may be able to help open up alcoholics and addicts

Interestingly, our animal companions aren't limited to cats, dogs, and horses. As romantic as the sound of "Horse Whisperer" is, therapy animals run the gamut from birds, to llamas and dolphins.

Although people use the term 'Animal Assisted Therapy' when using animals in a helping setting, you *are not* doing therapy. Using that term can place you in conflict with the legally regulated definition of "therapy." You are simply helping your prospect through the early days of staying clean and sober and providing them with an emotional support animal (ESA). ESAs often do the work of service and therapy—but more likely just their mere presence is beneficial. They help to:

a) open up a person who doesn't want to talk
b) relax someone when they begin to panic
c) allow them to focus on something other then their misery
d) make their helpers seem less threatening[32] you, in this case)
e) provide comfort and security in a threatening situation (newly off alcohol and drugs)

Factoid:[33] *There is a difference between Service Animals, Therapy Animals, Companion Animals and "Social/therapy" Animals. Some are certified via the Federal government, some are defined only in State Statutes. Owners may or may not be protected through various agencies.*

---

32 https://www.allaboutcounseling.com/forum/drug-addiction-treatment/emotional-support-animal-can-maintain-sobriety/
33 https://www.servicedogcertifications.org/difference-service-dog-emotional-support-animal/

The Mayo Clinic even recognizes the value of animals as a healing influence. They wrote about Pet therapy on their website in an article entitled, *Is medicine going to the dogs?*[34]

Pet therapy is a broad term that includes animal-assisted therapy and other animal-assisted activities. Animal-assisted therapy is a growing field that uses dogs or other animals to help people recover from or better cope with health problems, such as heart disease, cancer and mental health disorders.

Animal-assisted activities, on the other hand, have a more general purpose, such as providing comfort and enjoyment for nursing home residents.

As early as 1860 Florence Nightingale wrote in *Notes on Nursing*,[35] "A small pet animal is often an excellent companion for the sick, for long chronic cases especially. A pet bird in a cage is sometimes the only pleasure of an invalid confined for years to the same room. If he can feed and clean the animal himself, he ought always to be encouraged to do so."

Possibly you work at a small center and don't have the funding for equine or dolphin therapy. If you did, it would be a fantastic form of help for the newcomer. However, most of us do not have funds like that so we need to look at other animal options to build trust.

There is now a lot of evidence that not only do those that keep pets have better health but that putting animals into the care environment facilitates the entire process of healing—from trusting counselors to lowering depression and even blood pressure.

---

34 http://www.mayoclinic.org/healthy-living/consumer-health/in-depth/pet-therapy/art-20046342
35 http://digital.library.upenn.edu/women/nightingale/nursing/nursing.html

Factoid:[36] *Research shows that when people interact with a "therapy animal there is a significant drop in stress hormones such as cortisol, adrenaline and aldosterone and an increase in "health inducing and social inducing" hormones such as oxytocin, dopamine and endorphins."*

TRY using these animals:

BIRDS

Birds reduce depression,[37] boost moral, and lessen loneliness. In several studies of morale in older adults, the presence of a companion bird showed significant decreases in depression and loneliness. You wouldn't think that a bird could mean so much to seniors. But they actually do help. If you are reading this report for a center you work in or support, and they in no way will allow cats or dogs in the facility, birds are something you may be able to talk the regulators into. Look up the research before you approach the powers that be and carry it with you when you ask for pets to be included in the treatment setting. Use the term "emotional support animal" when you approach them.

Actually, crows may be as intelligent as chimpanzees.

---

36 http://psychcentral.com/lib/the-truth-about-animal-assisted-therapy/00010295
37 http://www.ncbi.nlm.nih.gov/pubmed/8839325

Factoid:[38] *New studies suggests that Crows, Ravens, and Jays are as intelligent as chimpanzees and gorillas. "Furthermore, crows may provide clues to understanding human intelligence. They say that crows and apes both think about their social and physical surroundings in complex ways, citing tool use as an example.*

Similarly, if you are in a residence setting that won't allow animals—you can often get away with a bird. Fish work to help calm people too—but they don't work on loneliness or trust issues.

DOGS & CATS

All sorts of pets seem to help their owners in times of stress, but dogs take first prize.[39] They provide companionship and become an object of attachment which gives meaning to life. We know that people who own pets, any pet, spend less time healing, make less doctor visits, and are generally more comforted in times of stress. But when looking closer at the research results, we find that dog owners spend more time with their pets and have deeper feelings of attachment for them and seem to have more companion benefits.

I remember writing a story about a formerly bad drug addict/biker named Wolf who had managed to eventually join a 12 Step program. He attributed his life to his dog who intervened when he tried to kill himself when coming off a drunk. Wolf had a shotgun to his mouth when his dog came up and lay his snout against his chest. Despite his internal

---

38 http://news.nationalgeographic.com/news/2004/12/1209_041209_crows_apes.html
39 http://www.ncbi.nlm.nih.gov/pubmed/2391640

suffering from his addiction, Wolf could not bring himself to do this and leave his dog behind.

Although for most people dogs work best, cats also lower blood pressure and trigger feelings of happiness in general. Sometimes people are more cat lovers and others are more dog lovers. Ideally, if you could get both animals in your center or home, you would have the best of both worlds.

PETS AS CO-FACILITATORS

Pets can serve as a co therapist for facilitation of rapport, providing emotional support and a sense of well-being. When presenting these suggestions at a conference for counselors, I had one psychiatrist, a recovering alcoholic himself, share his experience with dogs. He told my group that when he went through treatment, his facility had a house dog that the clients just loved. He recalled sitting with the dog for hours on end and actually talking and sharing his own troubles, things he could not bear to share in a group.

Dogs take first prize as ESAs

After gaining some sobriety and gong back to school for his doctorate, he began his own practice but never considered using a dog in the office, forgetting about his own positive experience. Eventually he got a puppy that was so young it could not be left alone at first. So he brought the retriever pup into the home office until it could be on its own. Immediately he noticed his clients responding to the pup, talking easier, trusting faster, and opening up in ways that could not be explained by his skills alone. He realized it was the puppy! Today, he would not dream of treating people with out his co-facilitator, Rufus.

RECAP

Even though you you may not be able to afford equine therapy or let the person you are helping swim with the dolphins, you can probably arrange for an emotional support animal for your prospect. As reported in the Eric Digests,[40] "Animals in counseling sessions and the classroom facilitate an atmosphere of trust, nurturance, and relationship building." A dog is likely to be the best bet if you are having trust issues. But birds will do if you are not allowed to introduce dogs or cats into the setting you find yourself in. Because of legal issues do not use the terms "therapy," "service animal" or any other therapeutic terms. Use the terms "Emotional Support Animal" (ESA) or "Animal-assisted Activities."

---

40 http://files.eric.ed.gov/fulltext/ED459404.pdf

Presenting Problem FOUR: Desperation & Helplessness

When people are desperate, in times of crisis and stress, seemingly random events take on undo significance. Under duress, the paranormal and spiritual beliefs that we may have thought ridiculous before, now taken on an aurora of power with predictive qualities. The daily horoscope speaks to us, having a psychic tell our future seems reasonable and exciting, random pages in a book about anger (especially when we were just angry) seems earth shatteringly directed at us. A talisman is quietly tucked into a pocket. Why? Because our minds are wounded and souls languish in fear. We have lost control. We grasp for control in a chaotic universe when we feel powerless. We must find meaning and order in our despair giving us hope to continue.

I have found when working with newly recovering alcoholics and addicts that in their search for control they grasp at anything that promises them a way to feel in control again. Those I worked with naturally gravitated toward signs and symbols, *anything* that would let them know the future or promise them success.

One of the more memorable events was a young man, Jim P., who was having a hell of a time staying clean and sober. He lived on skid row with a couple of other drunks and doubted he could make it. Yet Jim desperately wanted to. I had read somewhere that a psychic, Edgar Cayce, gave a recipe for "Mummy food" that was supposed to help drunks—it consisted of a cooked corn meal dish with dates. So I cooked some up for Jim. He latched onto this and j*ust knew* it would help him stay clean. When he was about to run out, he brought a quart jar to me and had me make another batch—and actually, he did stay clean. I wouldn't say it was the "Mummy food" from ancient Egypt, yet it did give him something to believe in, a little extra oomph that promised to make recovery easier. And the placebo effect apparently worked on him (unless there is something to the Mummy food!).

STRESS MAKES PEOPLE MORE SUPERSTITIOUS

Getting clean and sober is probably the hardest thing your prospect will ever have to do. When AA says, "It takes everything you have," they are not kidding. So to say people trying to detox are under "stress" is an understatement. In the Personality and Social Psychology Bulletin, Giora Keinan from Tel Aviv reported in her study of Stress and Desire for Control:[41]

> *Research shows that the frequency of magical thinking and superstitious behavior increases under conditions of stress. A possible explanation for this finding is that stress reduces the individual's sense of control and that to regain control she or he engages in magical rituals or superstitions.*

So what does this mean for you who are trying to help the newcomer in the first few months? It means you have another tool to use to tap into what is going on with them anyway. If you try to "get them to see" that reading the daily horoscope is pointless, you are like a fish swimming upstream. Use their natural bent toward magical thinking to help them help themselves. Go with the flow. Their subconscious will help you both. It knows what to tell this person that may help them reach their goal of sobriety. Let them "interpret things" and "see" meaning where you see none. Their subconscious is working to help your newcomer.

---

41 http://psp.sagepub.com/content/28/1/102.abstract.html

NOTE: There are many symbolic "oracles" you can use—so let the person you are helping choose what they like—don't try to "force" them to use dream interpretation or guided imagery if they find that juvenile. Read the following list to them and see what peaks their interest. Let your prospect chose what they like...this is *their* subconscious working again. Their subconscious will help them choose what works for them. And if they do not want to use any of these... (*or you don't*) just move on to other low cost low tech ways to help.

Susan Heitler, Ph.D. in *Psychology Today* wrote in her article "Resolution, Not Conflict (The guide to problem-solving)"[42]

We each, every one of us, do have subconscious knowledge of what we need to heal. To access that knowledge, that "sixth sense," though we need a way to enable the subconscious to speak.

Allow them to "see" meaning in random events.

---

42 http://www.psychologytoday.com/blog/resolution-not-conflict/201202/your-mind-has-extraordinary-powers

Using any of the methods listed here are the ways we enable our prospect's subconscious to work.

Don't fret that you may be aiding and abetting magical thinking. Once they have some sobriety under their belt and stabilize in their recovery, chances are pretty good their magical thinking will evaporate. It did with Jim P. He later became a respected businessman in his community and owned more than one treatment center. The magical belief that Egyptian Mummy food[43] was keeping him off booze did nothing to hurt and everything to help.

Here's how you let their fear of being out of control work for their benefit:

Recipe By Edgar Cayce
Serving Size : 4
-------- ------------ --------------------------------
1/2 Cup Dates,Chopped
1/2 Cup Black Mission Figs,Dried,Chopped
1 1/2 Cups Water
1 Tablespoon Cornmeal

1) Soak dates and figs overnight in water.
2) Cook in a saucepan over low heat, stirring constantly. Add corn meal slowly.

TRY THIS: Create Oracles

1. Dream Interpretation

Dreams are a gateway to the subconscious and anyone is able

---
43 http://i-40kitchen.blogspot.com/2010/11/vegan-mofo-day-12-mummy-food.html

to help themselves by learning to interpret their dreams. Early in the 20th century, as a culture, we began learning from Freud[44] and Jung[45] about how the subconscious tries to solve problems using the collective unconscious. Although I don't believe that *their* interpretations of other's subconscious use of symbols was particularly valid, I know that dreams help us grow and can be of therapeutic value in recovery.

I used dream interpretation in my own recovery and have even written several books about it, including one published by the A.R.E.[46] I give workshops and show counselors how to use dream interpretation with alcoholics and addicts. People who may not respond well to psychics or astrology often enjoy exploring their own dreams.

2. Guided imagery to overcome barriers

Guided imagery is sometimes called "imagineering." This is when a guide and an individual come together for the purpose of creating a new and insightful experience for the individual. If you are working in a treatment center, guided imagery is something you may want to add to your list of therapies if you are not using it already. It is particularly helpful because it helps people find their stumbling blocks in a an easy non-threatening way.

If you are a sponsor or caretaker using this manual, you may want to research this on the web...and find some interesting things to investigate about using imagery with your prospect —but only research it if they show interest.

Factoid:[47] *In a Study of 123 Marines by principal*

---
44 http://www.bartleby.com/285/
45 http://www.psychoheresy-aware.org/jungleg.html
46 http://www.edgarcayce.org/
47 https://medicalxpress.com/news/2012-09-ptsd-symptoms-combat-

investigator Dr. Mimi Guarner, it was found that healing touch and guided imagery is extremely effective in relieving symptoms of post-traumatic stress disorder (PTSD) in returning active duty military personnel, when combined with regular PTSD treatment.

Start with these sites to investigate using guided imagery for identifying recovery barriers in a non-threatening way:

a) **Guided imagery**[48] | There are no known contraindications for using guided imagery. This is not a technique, however, that should be incorporated into patient care when a client for personal or spiritual reasons is uncomfortable about using it. it is often described as **a stress management technique.**[49]

b) **FREE guided meditations**[50] | Fragrant *Heart* offers a whole list of MP3s that you can listen to for free to get started.

c) **Positive Change for Recovery from Addiction**[51] | Guided Meditation, a great one from YouTube.

d) **Sober Meditations**[52] | This website is focused on providing the recovering addict with help to relax, become more spiritually centered and enhance a healthy sober lifestyle through the use of guided video meditations and transformation meditation techniques.

Using guided imagery is most appropriate when a person is

---

exposed-military-medicine.html
48 https://www.psychologytoday.com/us/blog/integrative-mental-health-care/201808/guided-imagery-and-relaxation-therapy-anxiety
49 https://www.mindtools.com/pages/main/newMN_TCS.htm
50 https://www.fragrantheart.com/cms/free-audio-meditations
51 https://www.youtube.com/watch?v=mbQEu1LZW3U
52 http://www.sobermeditations.com/

inadequately coping with getting off alcohol and drugs, is in denial, is freaking out about personal relationships, or has self-destructive/self-sabotage behavior. If you do some exercises or explore digital recordings with them, the individual is the final word on the interpretation of any of the symbols. You, as a guide, only suggest things to examine. You may say something like, "If this were my journey I ...."

Helping with guided meditations

After guiding the person on the journey or after they listen to a recording, have them record the symbology. Use dream work techniques for interpreting the symbols. You are not a therapist so remember, they do the work, they do the interpretation, you just help them read the exercise or listen to a recording.

Guided imagery is fun—you may enjoy it too. You might think about both doing the exercise together and then discussing your own personal interpretations with each other.

3. Random openings of the basic texts

Have you ever had a problem and someone grabbed a book (usually a Bible) and had you close your eyes, open it randomly, and place your finger somewhere on the page? Then you read the passage under your finger and get the "answer" to whatever problem you had? This is one way to let the powers that be guide you to an answer.

Actually it works with almost any book because when someone is hurting and desperate, they attribute meaning even if there isn't any there. Reading random passages is a valid form of seeking help because the meaning you ascribe to the passage comes from *your* subconscious[53]—and is very likely contains the answer you need. Ascribing patterns and connections to random events is called apophenia and is a normal human experience.

The books you will want to use to randomly flip through will depend on what is your prospects drug of choice. Consider:

    Alcoholics Anonymous //amzn.to/2K4BAVx
    Narcotics Anonymous //amzn.to/2K3QZpb
    Chemically Dependents Anonymous //amzn.to/2I5RXz7
    Twelve and Twelve //amzn.to/2F1xDg6
    Serenity Bible //amzn.to/2I3UREc

If your prospect is a Christian with strong beliefs—definitely use the Bible and if they are Muslim then the Qur'an is in order. Use books that tie into their belief structure. *If they want to*. If you suggest something on this list and they turn up their nose—don't force it. These are just suggestions that you may find useful. Creating oracles is one of many tools. Some newly recovering people love them and others, not so much.

---

53 https://www.psychologytoday.com/us/blog/reality-check/201111/11-11-11-apophenia-and-the-meaning-life

As far as the books go, you may also want to consider recovery meditation books such as

Day by Day: Daily Meditations for Recovering Addicts //amzn.to/2K73Re0
Each Day a New Beginning: Daily Meditations for Women //amzn.to/2MA1nqM
Touchstones: A Book Of Daily Meditations For Men //amzn.to/2IxzHxD
Just for Today: Daily Meditations for Recovering Addicts //amzn.to/2IzuwgG
Pocket Sponsor, 24/7 Back to the Basics Support for Addiction Recovery //amzn.to/31j04Qh

To use this exercise, wait until your helpee is facing some problem, fear, or something that is agitating the hell out of them. Suggest they search for an answer by letting their higher self find an answer. If they seem interested, let your newcomer pick from a handful of books you keep handy for just such an occasion—recovery books, meditation books, religious or spiritual books.

Let their higher self find the answer

Have them close their eyes, hand over the book (upside down), and instruct them to open it randomly and run their finger down a page then stop when it "feels" right.

When they are done letting their higher self "find" the solution or inspiration they need, have them open their eyes, turn the book around and read. Ask your friend what it means and how this message may help with the given issue. Let *them* tell *you*. You'll be surprised at how targeted the solutions seem. And if your helpee wants to get clean and sober, their "answers" will reflect this.

4. Angel Jars: Pulling "messages" out of the jar

Like random passages from books, these are random messages from a compilations of messages in a jar. Call it an Angel Jar, Solution Box, Genie Jar—it is a container that carries messages, slogans, inspirational sayings—that are designed for a person to retrieve each day, week, or at the close of a meeting, whatever works.

This is a variation of daily affirmations but given a new framework, from a jar. Take any container and decorate it. Print one line recovery messages, slogans or affirmations you like. Take them from a recovery book—like slogans or ideas you like from Alcoholics Anonymous and print them in one or two lines (keep them brief with a single idea) Use heavier paper than for letters. If you use colored papers, all the better. Once they print, cut out the lines of text and fold. Put them in the container and decide when/how often they are to be used.

You can use jars, gift boxes, or even bags.

People often do "messages in a jar" for children—but the idea is great for therapy and recovery too. A variation of this is a Happiness Jar[54] inspired by Elizabeth Gilbert, the author of *Eat, Pray, Love*.[55] It's putting a good message *into* a jar to be pulled out later when in a funk.

Mason Jars work particularly well. They are plentiful and have a homey warm feeling to begin with. Here is a site that has some good examples of how to do them. Mason Jar Crafts[56]

5. A Few other Oracle Ideas

Random AA sayings scroll across their computer screen from Cybriety (screen saver to enforce recovery ideas)
//www.rewritables.net/cybriety/free_stuff!.htm
Get Big Book Bytes, a free app that downloads inspirational quotes from the Big Book, contains a sobriety tracker and allows you to share virtual sobriety tokens.
//www.pocketsponsor.com/
BigBookBytesApp/index.html
The Pocket Sponsor app is like an oracle of wisdom from the Old Timers in the 12 Step fellowships.
//www.pocketsponsor.com/PocketSponsorApp/
index.html
The pendulum can be thought of as an extension of the intuition, since it is used to gain access to information that exists at the subconscious level. Using a Pendulum to Enhance Intuition
//www.lovesedona.com/08.htm

Factoid:[57] *The saying "We Don't See Things As They Are, We See Them As We Are" has been attributed to*

---

54 http://www.wikihow.com/Keep-a-Happiness-Jar
55 https://amzn.to/2Wr8kKr
56 http://masonjarcraftsblog.com/inspiration-jars/
57 http://quoteinvestigator.com/2014/03/09/as-we-are/

Anaïs Nin. The Talmud. Immanuel Kant. G. T. W. Patrick. H. M. Tomlinson. Steven Covey. But no one truly knows its origin so it should be claimed as Anonymous.

<><><><><><><><>

RECAP

Allowing people who are desperate and trying to heal to give meaning to random events can be very helpful. Research has shown that people take comfort in seeing things as meaningful and significant to them in times of stress. From the American Psychological Association[58] we find the need to believe,

> *Adults also tend to search for meaning, particularly during times of uncertainty, research suggests. A 2008 study in Science (Vol. 322, No. 5898) by Jennifer Whitson, PhD, and Adam Galinsky, PhD, found that people were more likely to see patterns in a random display of dots if the researchers first primed them to feel that the participants had no control. This finding suggests that people are primed to see signs and patterns in the world around them, the researchers conclude.*

Allowing your prospect to ascribe meaning to events, random or not, is one path that helps them heal. In the long run, as solid recovery replaces the first few months—their need to read signs and symbols lessons. You can use their natural recovery process to work with, not against you, by simply allowing them to believe in things like Mummy food, if they so desire.

---

58 http://www.apa.org/monitor/2010/12/believe.aspx

Presenting Problem FIVE: Inability to focus, concentrate or retain information

In initial recovery trying to focus and concentrate on a single issue is very difficult. It is well known in recovery circles that a newcomer won't remember much of what goes on in the first few months. In addition, they fidget, wring their hands, can't sit still, and often don't track their thoughts well. Sometimes it is because they have the beginning stage of some type of brain damage. More often, it is simply the imbalance of neurotransmitters and the body misfiring as it tries to regain internal balance. I remember in my early recovery that sitting through an hour meeting was torturous. I *wanted* to sit still; I attempted to sit still so that it looked like I was making it; *I...could...not...do...it.* So my sympathy runs deep for the person trying to come off any mind affecting chemical who finds themselves constantly taking breaks from meetings even to the annoyance of those around him or her.

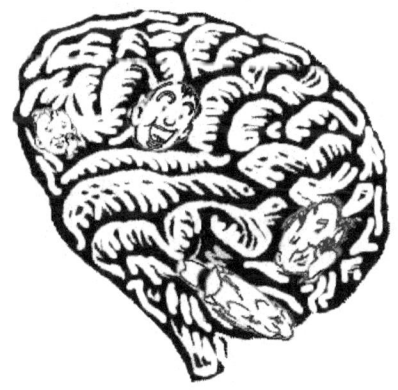

Brain regions shrink

<><><><><><><>

Factoid:[59] *Excessive alcohol consumption can result in*

---

59 http://www.plosone.org/article/info:doi/10.1371/journal.pone.0093586

a reduction of brain weight, with regional brain atrophy.

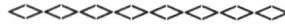

On the Prudent Opiate Practices & Psychological Services[60] website the problem of mind and concentration in early recovery is discussed:

> *There are several thought disorders experienced by a recovering person when PAW (Post Acute Withdrawal) is activated. Intelligence is not affected. It is as if the brain is malfunctioning sometimes. Sometimes it works all right. Sometimes is does not.*
>
> *One of the most common symptoms is the inability to concentrate for more than a few minutes. Impairment of abstract reasoning is another common symptom of post acute withdrawal. An abstraction is a nonconcrete idea or concept, something that you cannot hold in your hand, take a picture of, or put in a box. Concentration is more of a problem when abstract concepts are involved.*

So when your prospect can't sit through a whole movie, or forgets what they were yelling about 5 minutes before, or loses interest in your reading from a meditation book, *don't take it personally*. This is a rough time for them and they would probably pay more attention if they could. You don't want to make them feel any worse then they already do by getting upset over something they probably can't control. This is not to say, however, that they are not responsible for how they act. Having their mind wander during a conversation is one thing, but snapping at you in a disrespectful manner is another and not to be tolerated. In order for them to start recovery, they must begin to take responsibility for their choices. So don't let

---

60 http://www.poppswebsite.com/post-acute-withdrawal-paw/

them yell at you, call you names or be disrespectful. Be kind and caring but not a doormat.

TRY THIS: The 15 Minute Model

Keep most activities to around 15 minutes and repeat, repeat, repeat

> Remember the 15 Minute Rule. Give them nothing that requires their attention for longer than 15 minutes. For instance, if you need to review their upcoming schedule, make sure to break it down. Don't discuss their Doctor's appointment, Sunday at church, the visit from their Mom, and how they are going to pay the rent all in one setting. Begin with *one* of the issues. Discuss it, come to a conclusion, then have a cup of coffee. Or suggest a neck rub (you to them or them to you—let them do things for you if they can).

After a short period, tackle the next item. If anything can wait for the next day. Wait.

They will have trouble with their memory and concentration

Repeat everything. Even once you have settled something and create a schedule you both agree on, be sure to go over it several days in a row. They will have trouble with their memory and concentration. How much and for how long depends on how long they have been drinking or drugging and how their particular body reacts.

Do not snap, "I *told* you that three times," or I will be snapping at you, "I *told* you they will have trouble remembering!"

Repeating what you are doing and why you are doing it is helpful. Repeating positive recovery messages is helpful too. Maybe annoying at times, so annoying that they will be thinking you are driving them batty! Yet, being annoyed with you is part of the withdrawal process and is perfectly normal.

Keep reading/education activities brief and uncomplicated.

You may read a paragraph or two from something inspirational, then have a dialog. Let them make a phone call to a loved one (unless the loved one is part of the addiction problem; then rethink that one.)

Don't overwhelm a newcomer. Keep it simple.

Use brief and inspirational readings known as bibliotherapy. Remember, *you are not* a therapist, just a person reading inspirational things to the person you are helping. In beginning recovery even a whole page is often too much information to read or retain. Books, like the *Pocket Sponsor*,[61] or Hazelden's daily readers[62] can be helpful. AA has *24 Hours a Day*,[63] CDA has *Conscious Contact*,[64] and NA had *Just for Today*.[65] These are short, sweet and repetitive. These books use 12 Step spiritual concepts.

If your prospect just can't abide by any "God" talk or hates the 12 Steps (a decision I hope they will change their mind on someday) use alternative books. Emmet Fox's *Around the Year*[66] is very spiritual but not based on any 12 Step Fellowship. There are Zen inspirational readers, as well as other choices. Of course if they profess atheism, use something like *Beyond Belief*[67] musings for agnostics in recovery.

And don't forget audio books. From a website on how to make it through alcohol withdrawals,[68] they advise that "Reading a book is another option but some individuals may not have the concentration for this in early recovery. Audiobooks may be an effective solution for those who have trouble reading." With an audio book, their mind may wander in and out, and possibly a little bit of recovery will seep in, yet the experience will not overwhelm a person in detox

---

61 https://amzn.to/2ZleAF7
62 https://amzn.to/2KVnSnk
63 https://amzn.to/2KRySSq
64 https://amzn.to/2KTcYy9
65 https://amzn.to/2KTO8hJ
66 https://amzn.to/33SDRtP
67 https://amzn.to/33Wb2wh
68 https://alcoholrehab.com/alcoholism/how-to-make-it-through-alcohol-withdrawals/

because nothing is actively required of them.

Use every Recovery App for their phone you can find

Apps are wonderful things and if your prospect has a phone, put it to good use. (This includes tablets, iPads, and such.) Apps are generally designed to be brief with pointed information that does not waste your time. Most app programs are naturally segmented into small bytes of information. This is just what you are looking for.

The *Pocket Sponsor*[69] has an app I designed that gives out brief hourly meditations when you tap the icon. Hazelden has some great apps--ones that help you do a fourth step, some for their meditation books and so forth. Each is only a few dollars and worth the effort to give your prospect something to do that is easy, recovery-oriented and won't fluster them with complexities or deep thinking. A good free app is Big Book Bytes, in both iTunes and android markets.

The only exception to the 15 minute rule is movies and sports, which by their nature are continually active and moving. Movies change scenes often so the movie itself is already divided into segments. Even then, a lot of people in their first few months off alcohol and drugs find it difficult to sit through through a movie.

RECAP

Right now what you don't want to do is turn them off to recovery concepts. Since people going through a detoxification process tend to be spacy with the inability to concentrate, you need to keep them busy but not

---

69 http://www.pocketsponsor.com/app.html

overwhelmed. One sizable problem in many treatment centers is that they give newcomers too much too soon. The professionals know how much work the person has to do in their life to recover from addiction. So they try to give them as much as they can while they have them "captured" in treatment, but it usually backfires. Even professionals who *know* that the client won't retain much say things like, "But little bits of information seep in and will resurface when they need it." I'm not so sure that is true and suspect that overloading a person shaking off drugs may do more harm than good. Don't be so well meaning that you make this same mistake. Remember, busy, but segmented. Break all tasks into small segments and you will find your newcomer more cooperative and less agitated.

Presenting Problem SIX: Anger & Defiance

They have an "attitude;" they resent authority of any kind; they can't stand those assholes in AA. This is what leads to non compliance and will take your prospect right back to their drug of choice. Anger is a way alcoholics work themselves up and let the addiction make their choices for them. How many times have you heard something like, "If this happened to you, you would drink too!" When I worked in Russia the biggest excuse for drinking was, "If you had to live like we do you would drink too!" And I would have to remind them that we have just as many alcoholics in the US as they do in Russia.

Detoxifying individuals get angry at something/anything and if you don't go along, they get angry at you too. It is a form of 'madness' to let our emotions think for us and make our choices. Most of the time anger is caused because someone doesn't get their way, ie *they don't have control*. Even though addicts and alcoholics are wildly out of control, they want control...it is deep seated and permeates everything drunks do including withdrawal from mind-affecting mood-altering chemicals.

Watch for anger when they don't get their way

The behavior and absurdity (very real to the person going

through it) resemble that of a child--if I don't get my way I'll throw a tantrum, scream and yell and then gain back control. Or at least that is what their addict inside is telling them. You see, alcoholics and addicts don't have an inner child like the rest of the population. They have an inner addict and that inner addict will do anything it can to feed its obsession, their drug of choice. I use myself as an example when working with others because I lived with this inner addict until its anger and choices almost killed me. And I was only 21.

Sobriety Police

So your job, when supporting the person trying to get clean and sober, is to "trick, cajole, and be stern" with that inner addict--a daunting task. You don't want them seeing you as the sobriety police and their enemy. One way to ease a person's defiance, anger and need for control is to give them more control, not take it away.

The Montessori schools[70] use a slick method where they define certain parameters and then have their pupils make their own choice within those parameters. They don't want frustrated kids that follow rigid rules--they want creative and happy kids. So their solution is to give their students the feeling of controlling their own lives and destiny by giving them more choice--instead of dictating what to study they give them choices within a predetermined and suitable parameter. For instance, a young girl of say three or four may want to

---

70 http://ageofmontessori.org/montessori-and-freedom-of-choice/

wear inappropriate clothes to church--like a bathing suit or a Halloween costume and they don't want *you* to tell *them* what to wear; they want to exert their independence. If you force them to wear what you pick out week after week it stifles creativity, causes rebellion and increases anger.

The Montessori solution is for a parent to lay out several suitable dresses and then ask the child, "Which one do you want to wear today?" Delighted, the child makes a choice, changes her mind, makes another choice, and finally settles on something. This way, the girl doesn't feel oppressed or disregarded but a central part of her own life decisions.

Factoid:[71] *Montessori's biographer E.M. Standing suggests that freedom to choose is not freedom to do anything you want, but freedom to do the right thing.*

Dealing with the inner addict of your prospect will be much the same. If all you do is become the "No No" person and they feel you are forcing them to stay sober, their recovery isn't going to happen. The very best way to help your prospect deal with their inner addict is to give them more choices so they are invested in what is happening to them.

TRY THIS: Give them Choices

One of the first things I do is help the person pick out what type of literature is the best fit for them, which support group they will accept, and which program resonates with them. Is it AA, NA, Alcoholic's Victorious, Smart Recovery? Most people will end up in AA if they are to remain sober, even those that despise it at first. Yet, they don't have to be forced by you; they can make their own initial decisions. When

---

71 http://ageofmontessori.org/montessori-and-freedom-of-choice/

people make their own decisions they are more apt to follow through. They have some investment in it. If you make all their decisions, they could care less about following through.

The 12 Step Fellowships have people pick their own sponsors. It becomes a sacred ritual for most. Who is going to help me best? Newcomers use all sorts of methods for finding "just the right" person to be their sponsor. When a newcomer does finally ask someone, they are much more likely to listen to their choice then if they were assigned some one when they walked in the door.

Treatment centers would do well to let new clients do the same--pick their own counselor. They could give their newly admitted client a brief period to adjust and then, by say, five days, pick the person on the staff they want to counsel them. The client is much more likely to be happy with their treatment if they pick their own counselor. Even putting counselor names in a hat and having a client pick randomly would have a greater positive response than having a counselor assigned to them. (see Presenting Problem Four about oracles)

I developed a simple Questionnaire which can help a person choose which basic text they think will help them and which support program they would prefer. This Questionnaire was originally was published in *Sober Coaching Your Teen* and is now available to you in a PDF file. You may download and print it out so that you can easily use it with your prospect.[72]

You can review the questionnaire, but it would be best if you actually printed it out and have your friend fill it out. After answering the questions, there is a summery of the strong points and weak points of the types of support available for recovery. This is NOT intended for you to pick the program

---

72 http://www.pocketsponsor.com/PDF/Questionnaire-ProgramType.pdf

they should join. As their support person you are now a type of Sober Coach and you can locate the resources or help your charge locate them but let them pick the resources they want. This questionnaire is intended to give you an overview so you can respect and support the choice they make once they finish.

Self-Help Programs. Which is best for You?

Questionnaire

1. Answer the Assessment Questions
2. Tally the Answers
3. Discover the Best Self-help Program and Recovery Book for You
4. Order Your Basic Texts

PART ONE: QUESTIONS

Below are a number of situations for you to review. Circle the letter of the statement that best describes your position. You may agree with more than one, but only circle the description that seems more important then the others.

There are no right or wrong answers. This is designed to help you decide what type of literature and self-help group will most aid you in recovery. Don't write in answers you think others might like to see, like your counselor, parents, or spouse. Just check the responses that describe who *you really are*.

Circle one in each category:

1. <u>The type of people I prefer to associate with are people who:</u>
    a) Are open-minded, non-judgmental, and able to
    b) appreciate my good qualities
    c) Are real-life survivors that are not afraid to tell it like it is
    d) Have been around, know the score, and are confident in how they dress and act
    e) Live by Faith-based principles
    f) Will let me talk about my feelings and are conscious of micro aggressions
    g) Do well in school or at work, are logical, and do more than party and worry about social media

2. <u>When dealing with problems, I prefer to solve them by:</u>
    a) Listening to how others have faced the same thing and then solve the problem for myself
    b) Following clear directions, but only by people who know what the hell they're doing
    c) Watching others do things, discuss it with my friends, then make my own decision.
    d) Praying and then accepting guidance from my minister if appropriate
    e) Looking at how successful women faced the same problems in their lives (Mom, Grandmother, Elders, and political figures I admire)
    f) Asking a teacher, professor or some other authority

figure that can provide facts so I can figure it out myself

3. <u>When it comes to religious matters:</u>
   a) I am open-minded about God and religion and respect other's choices.
   b) I have my own ideas about God and don't mind letting others know what I think.
   c) All things spiritual fascinate me, like the world religions including Tantra Yoga, Martial Arts, Wicka, indiginous teachings, and the supernatural.
   d) I choose the dominion of my religion and call my Higher Power by His real name (ie Jesus Christ, Allah)
   e) One problem I have with religion is when they say women have to be subservient to men.
   f) It isn't logical to seek a "god" or higher power if you are scientifically literate.

4. <u>I would prefer to socialize with and am most comfortable with:</u>.
   a) People of all ages who are responsible and do what they say they are going to
   b) Real, down to earth people who basically mind their own business
   c) Energetic people who won't let anything hold them back from participating fully in life and love
   d) The fellowship of those who participate in my faith and have values like me
   e) Women who are competent, self-assured, and not dependent on others to define them
   f) Intellectual and successful people who don't go around proselytizing about anything

5. <u>These sets of words most closely describe what I like:</u>

LIFE:
   a) A stable, joyous life

b) An exciting, even if risky, life
c) A just life, with protections for all
d) A devout life
e) A caring and sharing life
f) A no-nonsense, self-determined life

MEDIA: I ENJOY A CROSS SECTION OF

a) Reality TV, dramas, series, news, movies, and some family Facebook and Twitter
b) Action films, comedy sitcoms, reality shows, weather channel, cop reality shows and series, YouTube, Facebook groups, maybe a bit of Twitter and Instagram, radio
c) MTV, thriller films, Entertainment Tonight, Sci Fi, YouTube, Instagram and Snapchat
d) Family entertainment, contemporary cartoons, animal shows, evening news. and faith-based entertainment
e) Romantic films, animal rescue shows, extreme makeovers, PBS, morning talk shows, music on the radio. some family Facebook and groups, and Twitter
f) True stories, Discovery, investigative dramas, FBI files, talk radio, YouTube, alternative news like BBC

FOOD:

a) I don't like to make a big deal out of what I eat but am conscious of the food pyramid and use the guidelines of the American Heart Association
b) I listen to my physician, sometimes do Keto or other strict diets as long as it is not tofu and brown rice, love BBQs and buffets
c) Whatever works: Keto, pizza, vegan, fancy food, sugarless, basically whatever my friends are into and I don't have to obsess over what I'm eating
d) Home-cooked meals like Grandma and Mom make, pot lucks, BBQs
e) I try not to eat too much and use organic when I can, probably obsess on my diet now and again, and

      confess to following fads with diets for health and weight control
      f) Any combination that provides a nourishing, solid diet

PERSONAL SPACE:
      a) I don't worry about the "personal space" thing
      b) Personal space? Let's just say, "Don't get in my face..."
      c) I encourage everyone (including myself) to be aware and not trigger others
      d) We are all brothers and sisters
      e) My best friends are always allowed into my personal space
      f) I insist on my own space

WORK:
      a) Getting a job is a good thing so I can take care of myself and family
      b) I only do work I enjoy; if I don't like it, "Take this job and shove it."
      c) I would never work at anything gross plus I need a healthy paycheck
      d) If I do what I am supposed to each day, the right work will come
      e) I believe in equal pay for equal work with men and women
      f) If I want something, I expect to compete for it, including a job

VALUES:
      a) Most people know right from wrong and I want to do the right thing
      b) I honor the code of the people I am with
      c) I am unique, woke, and can express my values while being sensitive to others
      d) Grace and guidance from my faith are the only standards I am interested in
      e) People are basically good and that includes me

f) I believe in the separation of church and state, the Pledge of Allegiance should not contain "Under God," and truth is relative

Tally Your Answers

Please tally up your choices of a's, b's, etc. Count and record what you picked.

A____ B____ C____ D____ E____ F____

Read the section or sections below that you checked most often. This will help you decide which of the self-help programs fits your personality type. Once you go to several meetings in your category, you may want to order the basic text of that group to help you stay abstinent. Often you will not find these meetings in your community other than AA or NA. If that is the case, look up meetings on line for the program that best suits you and begin attending virtual meetings. Also, attend AA and NA to see how they are run. Once you understand the basics and have some recovery behind you, it will be time to start a recovery meeting of the program of your choice if there isn't one in your area. After all, someone has to do it, so it may as well be you!

PART TWO: INTERPRETING YOUR ANSWERS

Discover the Best Self-help Program for You

The A Responses: ALCOHOLIC'S ANONYMOUS[73]

Mostly A's indicate that you would fit in with the type of people that go to Alcoholic's Anonymous. AA is a life-time program based on staying clean and sober and doing the next right thing.

---

73 https://www.aa.org/

Generally speaking, people who go to AA share middle-American values. Some minorities feel that AA doesn't address enough subgroups. In answer to this, many specialty groups have formed in AA like young people's groups, gay and trans, men's or women's, indigenous, biker's, African-American, Hispanic, and even metaphysical groups.

AA is the first 12 Step program and thus the parent of all subsequent 12 Step programs. Often you will belong to another recovery organization for specific and personal interests and belong to AA as a type of anchor in your clean and sober program.

AA's strong points: They have the most varied experience in recovery, the majority of members in recovery, the smoothest running organization world wide, and the strongest social network. AA meetings can be found almost anywhere in the world and certainly everywhere in the US. AA is a fellowship that reaches out to those in trouble in a way so powerful and dedicated that millions of lives have been saved. They also have the most young people's groups.

AA's weak points: Although AA was the first to introduce the disease concept of alcoholism, they have a tendency to see alcohol as different from other mind-affecting chemicals. Members admit that one can't use other drugs, but some members still discourage "drug talk" even though it directly relates to a person's drinking. For addicts whose drug of choice was other then alcohol, you can sometimes be made to feel uncomfortable. AA's "traditional" understanding of the disease of addiction is limited.

The basic text of AA is a book called ***Alcoholic's Anonymous.***[74] This is the book you will order if you picked mostly A's in the assessment form. If you are under age 25,

---

74 https://amzn.to/2Kv9TnU

you should read the section for "C" responses and consider ordering *Young, Sober, & Free*[75] or *Chemically Dependent Anonymous*[76] as your basic text.

The B Responses: NARCOTIC'S ANONYMOUS[77]

Mostly B responses would indicate that you would fit in well with the type of people that attend Narcotic's Anonymous. Although the name is "Narcotic's", the program actually address the disease of addiction from any mind-effecting chemical. Like AA this is a program based on staying clean and sober and doing the right thing. NA generally has more streetwise, hard-core addicts in recovery rather than the more mainstreamed middle-class folks of AA. For rebellious/fiercely independent people that seemed to be on the wrong side of the law, lived on the streets, are rather eccentric, or dealt with the drug runners, NA may be a better choice than AA for you. At least at first. If you used mainly marijuana you will also want to find a **Marijuana Anonymous**[78] group. If you were a crack user, you will want to find a **Cocaine Anonymous**[79] group in addition to NA and AA. There is even a **Crystal Meth Anonymous**[80] self-help organization.

The strong points of NA: People in NA address the disease of addiction rather than a specific chemical. In AA the first step addresses "alcohol" and in NA the first step address the disease of "addiction." People in NA understand addiction better and know why they can't use any mind-affecting chemicals.

---

75 https://amzn.to/2KMpkam
76 https://amzn.to/2H0ma1y
77 https://na.org/
78 https://www.marijuana-anonymous.org/
79 https://ca.org/
80 https://crystalmeth.org/index.php

The weak points of NA: NA has become so generic in referring to drugs that members, in many instances, are not allowed to talk about their specific drugs of choice or give details about their use. A member can't say I'm a "coke head" or "junkie", but are often required to say "addict." The rules and standards of behavior have become very oppressive in NA--so only those that can withstand very strong guidance and strict standards of behavior should make NA their exclusive program.

The book for those that answered with mostly "B's" will be *Narcotic's Anonymous*.[81] Even though the NA groups are dictatorial in their approach to recovery right now, their basic text is not. It is much clearer then the AA book when it comes to addiction and what that means. Unfortunately, it doesn't have the great personal examples that AA does. Later, you may want to pick up the AA text, but for hard-core users, this is the basic text to start with. For pot heads try *Life with Hope*[82] and for cocaine addicts you will want *Hope, Faith & Courage: Stories from the Fellowship of Cocaine Anonymous.*[83]

The C Responses or a mixture of AB&Cs: YES GROUPS[84] & CHEMICALLY DEPENDENT ANONYMOUS[85]

Regardless of your primary drug of choice, if you checked mostly "C" responses or have an even mixture of A, B, &Cs, you are a good candidate for joining CDA as well as continuing to go to other support groups. There is no program per se for young people in recovery, but CDA will probably be the best choice. There are young people found in Young People's groups within AA ,NA, CA, and other self-help

---

81 https://amzn.to/2Z3O1nO
82 https://amzn.to/33vrL9x
83 https://amzn.to/2H7s40L
84 https://www.nyintergroup.org/meetings/youth-enjoying-sobriety-y-e-s/
85 https://www.cdaweb.org/

groups. In California and Arizona, there are the "YES" groups (Youth Enjoying Sobriety) which can be contacted through local AA service offices.

If you are a young person, you are encouraged to form relationships with all ages in recovery. You also need to identify with others in your age group. People as young as nine have come to recovery groups. There are now thousands of people who began recovery from age 12 to 19 who have 15 to 25 years without using mind-effecting chemicals. Don't ever let anyone tell you that you are too young to be in recovery. How young do you have to be to die? How old do you have to be to live?

Chemically Dependent Anonymous is the tolerant and loving response to AA and NAs reluctance to embrace the new addict who recognizes the true nature of drug addiction. Alcoholics Anonymous has been lovingly tolerant of these new drug dependents, so long as they express the desire to stop using alcohol. But, flexible as the AA program is, it can only bend so far before it begins to pose a threat to its own traditional structure. Narcotics Anonymous has not been so tolerant. If you don't speak, dress, and think the partly line you are pretty much told to leave.

The strong points of CDA: CDA refuses to make distinctions, between dope fiends, drug addicts, pot heads, prescription pill poppers and alcoholics in the important aspects of the recovery process. They tell you to use whatever literature works, go to any 12 Step programs you want to, and they don't force you to obey rules about what you can say or do. In CDA you can tell your whole story without fearing censorship or critical attitudes. If available (mostly on the east coast), CDA is a great choice.

The weak points of CDA: They are not well known at this point and have limited meetings in the country. So support is not as prevalent as AA and NA, yet they rely heavily on those programs so getting a copy of the ***CDA book***[86] to refer to while attending other 12 step group meetings is a good idea too.

If you picked mostly "C's" or you picked "A's" and "B's" but are under 25, you will want to use the basic text ***Young, Sober, & Free***[87] and ***Chemically Dependent Anonymous.***[88] These text's explain the disease of addiction in a clear, concise and contemporary manner. As with all of the basic texts, there are personal stories that you will be able to identify with.

The D Responses: FAITH-BASED SUPPORT such as OVERCOMERS OUTREACH,[89] ALCOHOLIC'S VICTORIOUS,[90] CELEBRATE RECOVERY,[91] AND MILLATI ISLAMI[92]

The programs that are most suitable for those with deep faith-based convictions will be Overcomers Outreach, Alcoholic's for Christ, Alcoholic's Victorious, Celebrate Recovery and Millati Islami. Many traditional faiths believe that drinking is a sin or at least overindulgence is. These are 12 Step programs based on the Bible or Qur'an. The majority of the faith-based programs act to bridge the gap between traditional 12 Step groups and their spiritual teachings. They meet in religious fellowship and usually call their Higher Power, Jesus Christ or in the case of Millati Isami, Allah. The groups are run by lay people, as are all the 12 Step programs and they seek to integrate the spheres of both their religious teachings and the Twelve Step approach to recovery in a simultaneous program.

---

86 https://amzn.to/2H0ma1y
87 https://amzn.to/2KMpkam
88 https://amzn.to/2H0ma1y
89 https://overcomersoutreach.org/
90 https://www.alcoholicsvictorious.org/
91 https://www.celebraterecovery.com/
92 http://www.millatiislami.org/

The strong points about Faith-based groups: If you are a deeply devout person and suffer from guilt and shame from your alcoholism and addiction, you may be reluctant to attend all-inclusive community support. Fortunately, you will find anonymity and spiritual healing in these faith-based groups. Honest sharing is encouraged without condemnation and members are offered a program of recovery that blends with religious leanings. These programs combine the best of 12 Step recovery with the best disciplines from your own faith.

The weak points about Faith-based groups: Overcomers Outreach and Celebrate Recovery deal with all addictions (this is not true for the other groups), compulsions, and problems and is not just for drug addictions. This waters down the effectiveness for addicts and alcoholics. Alcoholics for Christ, of course is just for alcoholics and would not be as comprehensive for understanding the true nature of drug addiction that accompanies alcoholism. These groups are not as widespread or easy to find as AA and NA. In any case, you may want to supplement your Faith-based group with the experience and fellowship from other 12 Step recovery groups.

For those who wish to include their faith in their addiction recovery, their basic text will be recommended by their respective group. ***A Bridge to Recovery***[93] is one of the books I recommend. This book describes the healing powers of Jesus Christ and the miracles He brings to those who practice the 12 Steps. It reveals that addiction is not a sin but a disease of the body, mind, and spirit. Another good resource is the ***Serenity Bible.***[94]

---

93 https://amzn.to/2H1nRvr
94 https://amzn.to/2yRo53R

The E Responses: WOMEN IN SOBRIETY[95]

For women who checked many of the E responses, you will be very comfortable in the Women For Sobriety groups. This is not a 12 Step program but a cognitive type approach to recovery based on abstinence, growing emotionally, and empowering yourself. WFS members take great pride in being female and stress their sober attributes by saying, "We are capable and competent, caring and compassionate, always willing to help another; bonded together in overcoming our addictions." WFS deals exclusively with the special needs, struggles, and issues of women in recovery.

The strong points of WFS: For women who have felt belittled and been abused, these groups are a liberating and feel-good approach to recovery. Rather then focusing on the past, they look to the future to build emotional strength, self-esteem, and positive approaches to life. The web site begins by giving women13 Acceptance Statements and this kind of support is especially good if you were sexually abused as a child or exploited in your drugging and drinking life.

The weak points of WFS: Like the other lesser-known recovery groups, these women can be hard to find and there are few groups for support. In addition, the attitude that women need "special" considerations can have a negative effect like that for young people's groups--"I'm different therefore I can't be helped."

For women who need more nurturing from other women or who are staunch feminists and cannot imagine a guy-influenced support system, WFS is an approach you may want to take. Your basic text will be the book ***Goodbye Hangovers, Hello Life.***[96]

---

95 https://womenforsobriety.org/
96 https://amzn.to/2KuEVME

The F Responses: SOS SOBRIETY: THE PROVEN ALTERNATIVE TO 12 STEP PROGRAMS[97]

If you cannot imagine relying on any religious or spiritual program to pull you out of this affliction, SOS The Secular Organization for Sobriety might suit you. Secular Organizations for Sobriety (also known as "Save Our Selves"), claims it is the world's largest non-12 Step addiction recovery program. SOS is an alternative recovery method for those young people who are uncomfortable with the spiritual content of widely available 12 Step programs. SOS credits the individual for achieving and maintaining his or her own sobriety, without reliance on any "Higher Power."

The strong points of SOS: SOS respects recovery in any form regardless of the path by which it is achieved. It is not opposed to or in competition with any other recovery programs. For people who do not want to combine spirituality with their program or have tried AA and didn't like it, SOS can present a new lease on recovery. SOS supports healthy skepticism and encourages the use of the scientific method to understand chemical dependency.

The weak points of SOS: Although SOS does believe addiction is a disease, they don't go in much for the therapies and counselor-based support. They believe that addiction is independent of any other life problems. Also, they do not have the widespread support that AA, NA, and CA enjoy. But over 300 meetings worldwide isn't bad.

Individuals who checked a lot of "F's" will want to use *SOS Sobriety: The Proven Alternative to 12-Step Programs*[98] as their basic text. Like the other basic texts, it discusses what

---

97 http://www.sossobriety.org/
98 https://amzn.to/31ESOgO

addiction is, what you can do about it, and gives personal examples of how the system works.

RECAP

Anger usually stems from people not getting their own way. Another way to look at it is to say they cannot control people, places, and things and when unable to make things go their way, they get mad. Although the experience of the person detoxing is very real, and their anger justified in their own minds, you are basically dealing with a child in the body of a willful and irrational grownup. One way to make it so they don't feel so helpless is to give them control by giving them choices. Don't become the Sobriety Police, dictating what they must do at every turn.

Much the same as the Montessori philosophy, give your helpee choices from a suitable framework. Let them pick the recovery literature they want. Ask when they prefer to do a quiet meditation, before coffee, after, or before the evening meal? What support group will they join? Maybe they can't at this time go to an in-person meeting, then help them find an Internet group. Give them choices and you take away some of the those feelings of helplessness that lead to anger and defiance. They invest themselves in their own recovery plan and are much more likely to cooperate with you.

Presenting Problem SEVEN: Self pity & Hopelessness

"This can't work for me; why me? I have all the bad luck." On page 84 of the book Alcoholics Anonymous, the promises of recovery are discussed. One of them is, "That feeling of uselessness and self-pity will disappear." That promise does come true for most people who quit drinking, but in the first few months, it is anything but.

What bad luck, a newcomer asks himself, to have this horrible disease. They think of all those in their life that don't suffer from alcoholism and addiction and believe it was themselves that got the tough breaks. Yet alcoholics go through years, sometimes decades doing the same destructive behavior, trying to control the outcome and *it just doesn't work.* Instead of realizing that they are at the root of their own troubles, they blame anything and everything eventually landing on the belief its just plane rotten luck.

Why me?

But the great thing about the addictive diseases is that the treatment is so very simple, just don't pick up the FIRST one. Of course it escapes newcomers as anyone trying to help them probably already knows. I mean if we alkies took responsibility at the first signs of trouble with our drinking and drugging, would the relapse rate be so high?

Poor me, Poor me, Pour me a drink.

So what is your job in assisting this person when you hear them whining with self pity?

TRY THIS: Teach them to ask the right questions:

Alcoholics and addicts have a tendency to be trapped in their own insanity of dependence. We often say of ourselves that we keep doing the same thing over and over again expecting a different result. Oh how we resist change. But those of us who have maintained some clean and sober time know that change we must! Some sponsors in recovery tell their sponsees that they only have to change *everything*. Well, in the first few months we don't need to frighten our prospect with quite so drastic a message. We can begin with one small warmup in making change: teach them to ask solution-oriented questions, not hopeless and helpless questions.

From the book, **Do One Thing Different**[99], Bill O'Hanlon, often has folks change the questions they ask. It helps change the thinking. Remember if addicts and alcoholics are to recover they must change what? Everything!

> **Ask Different Questions:** The quality of your questions determines the quality of your results, so make sure that you are asking the right questions. If the questions you ask in a situation do not get you what you want, reframe your

---

99 https://amzn.to/2ZgZxRo

questions and/or evaluate your situation and think of better questions to ask. *From a book review about one of Bill's books at the Invisible Mentor*[100]

Problem Questions:

    ask for explanations, place blame, but keep you stuck
    make you feel helpless and victimized

Solution Questions:

    require action to change a situation
    open up new possibilities

Change Problem Questions to Solution Questions

As a general rule, "Why" Questions tend to lead to self-pity, not self actualization

    Why did this happen to me?
    Why did the courts send me to treatment?
    Why did my wife leave me?
    Why am I an addict?

As a general rule "How" questions tend to be solution oriented

    How can I turn this into a positive experience?
    How can I use treatment to my best advantage?
    How can I become the man whom I will love and respect?
    How can my addiction be stopped?

---

100 http://theinvisiblementor.com/the-change-your-life-book-by-bill-ohanlon-a-book-review/

Ask the right question

RECAP

When your charge gets into the blaming and self pity mode, refereed to as the "pity pot" in AA, a little bit of sympathy might be in order, but don't give their negative emotion too much energy. They have been blaming people, places, and things for a long time and part of recovery is fessing up to our part in events. You may want to explain the difference between "problem" questions (the questions that keep you stuck) and solution-oriented questions. Have them reframe their questions and see if they can't get off that pity pot.

Presenting Problem EIGHT: Fear, Panic, Dread

When I first stopped drinking and using drugs (hippie child that I was), fear become a constant companion. Suddenly I faced the world with no chemical buffer and every fear from my childhood, starting with goblins under the bed to spooky entities in the dark, sprang back to haunt me. When I drove to my support groups and stepped out of my car, I was convinced that a rattlesnake might have slithered under the car and would strike as I walked to my meeting.

Even then, I knew how insane and irrational this was but I could not shake the fear. It was difficult to sleep at night for fear of spirits taking over my body. No matter how rationally I talked to myself, the fear sometimes paralyzed me. Do NOT poo poo the newcomer's irrational thoughts, fears, and dread. It is very real to them. Help them find a way to still their rabid thoughts and slow down that inner addict dialog that is out to kill them. This can only be achieved through discipline of the mind and emotions. That is why serenity is so important in the early days. The Serenity Prayer was a huge form of support for me. I repeated it so often it became like a mantra: *God grant me the serenity...* And for a long time, that prayer served as my form of daily meditation.

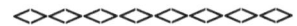

Factoid:[101] *In 1939, an obituary came to the attention of an early AA member, Jack, who had spotted it in the New York Times. It read:*

Mother, God grant me the serenity to accept things I

101http://open-mind.org/Serenity.htm

cannot change, courage to change things I can, and wisdom to know the difference. Goodbye.

Jack brought this obituary to the AA office and the simple prayer reflected the fledglings organization's values so deeply that they printed up 500 wallet-sized cards with today's version.

How do you help them create the discipline they need to help still the fear and dread?

TRY THIS: Meditation

Those who meditate develop a greater love and acceptance for their own humanity. Their spiritual challenge is to find the sacred within the mundane. Meditation calms down the innards and provides a connection to our spiritual awareness, often a Higher Power, or at the very least a deep calm and connection to humanity. It also quiets the mind makes room for solution oriented thoughts instead of constant "defense" thoughts.

More meditations exist than you can imagine. Many people think they don't like to meditate, yet I bet they do. If you only think meditation is siting cross legged on a mat with your thumb and index creating a circle or laying prone and relaxing muscles from your toes up to your eyeballs, you are missing the fun ways to meditate. There really is a Meditation Model for everyone.

Factoid:[102] *According to reports, there have been over 1500 separate studies since 1930. All were related to*

102http://www.project-
    meditation.org/a_wim1/statistics_on_people_who_meditate.html

meditation and its effects on the practitioners. Some statistics on people who meditate include results like:

Meditators are less anxious and nervous.
Meditators were more independent and self-confident
People who deliberated daily were less fearful of death.
75% of insomniacs who started a daily meditation program were able to fall asleep within 20 minutes of going to bed.
Production of the stress hormone Cortisol is greatly decreased, thus making it possible for those people to deal with stress better when it occurs.
Women with PMS showed symptom improvements after 5 months of steady daily rumination and reflection.
Thickness of the artery walls decreased which effectively lowers the risk of heart attack or stroke by 8% to 15%.

Keep in mind that this technique works hand in hand for technique Six: Anger & Defiance. Letting your prospect pick the type of meditation they are willing to do is a wonderful opportunity to give Choices again.

Meditation Models to chose from

Art As Meditation
//arttherapyreflections.blogspot.com/2012/01/why-is-art-making-form-of-meditation.html
Breath Meditation
//breathmeditation.org/the-breath-of-life-the-practice-of-breath-meditation
Concentration Meditation
self-guided.com/concentration-meditation.html
Dance Meditation   (this is on YouTube)
youtube.com/watch?v=7L7xwKQjVSs
Grounding
project-meditation.org/mt/grounding_meditation.html

Group Meditation
spiritscienceandmetaphysics.com/proof-that-group-meditation-can-change-the-world/
Guided Meditation
//marc.ucla.edu/body.cfm?id=22
Mandalas
mandala-4u.com/en/start.html
Mantras
//owen.curezone.com/spirituality/sanskrithealing.html
Martial Arts
danzanryu.com/qigong.html
Mindfulness
psychologytoday.com/blog/the-courage-be-present/201001/how-practice-mindfulness-meditation
Movement Meditation
beliefnet.com/Faiths/Faith-Tools/Meditation/2000/12/Movement-Meditation.aspx
Noting Meditation
buddhistgeeks.com/2011/07/mahamudra-noting/
Rituals (like prayer, saying the Rosary)
//healing.about.com/od/higherselfmeditate/a/yeh_dailyritual.htm
Sensory Awareness
trans4mind.com/jamesharveystout/sensory.htm
Spiritual Practice In Daily Life
ignatianspirituality.com/ignatian-prayer/the-spiritual-exercises/
Sports Meditation
theorderoftime.com/politics/cemetery/stout/h/sportsme.htm
Visualization Meditation
youtube.com/watch?v=wVt_WmUHSNQ
Walking Meditation (a Medicine Wheel can also be a walking meditation) meditationoasis.com/how-to-meditate/simple-meditations/walking-meditation/
Witnessing Your Thoughts
swamij.com/witnessing.htm

◇◇◇◇◇◇◇◇
NOTE: *Putting links to these various forms of meditations does not imply an endorsement of any of the methods or attest to its suitability to a particular person. The links are for educational purposes only.*
◇◇◇◇◇◇◇◇

Walking Meditation

When working with a young person, you will find they often gravitate toward dancing meditations and sports meditations. This doesn't mean that you take them to a night club so they can meditate! You do it in an isolated place with no distractions. Dance meditation can be slow and deliberate such as ballet exercises or fast and twirling like the whirling dervishes of the Sufi.[103] Have them pick a principle to focus on as they dance or have them try to clear their minds and think of nothing. Sports meditation is a repetitive movement such as dribbling a basket ball and holding a thought or doing situps with the thought.

---

103 http://veryethnic.com/2012/06/29/13-things-the-whirling-dervishes-can-teach-you-about-spinning-until-youre-dizzy-enough-to-puke/

Meditating does not have to be laying prone and relaxing each body part. It is methodical and repetitive while holding a single thought or conversely no thought. It is a way to clear the mind and bring discipline to self. It is any method that takes everyday distractions out of the mind and emotions if just for a few moments. Go over the different ways to meditate and have your charge find which one works for them.

A freebie from Real Meditation for Real Alcoholics:[104] *Real Meditation for Real Alcoholics - and those who love them" introduces readers to a special, non-religious, mindful meditation technique. It is a unique method that does not clash with the fundamental spiritual Principles laid into the recovery foundation of many recovered or "recovering" alcoholics*

Any of the above will work. The basics you apply are this:[105]

a) make it repetitive
b) have them 'clear' the mind and focus on a single thing, usually a recovery precept or spiritual principle (many people suggest clearing the mind entirely and think of nothing)
c) begin with a few minutes--from three to five--then increase the time slowly to a level they are comfortable with

RECAP

Alcoholics and addicts are not stable in early recovery. Sometimes they put on a brave front but in AA they say newcomers are like a "boy whistling in the dark to keep up his

---

104 http://stepelevencomesalive.blogspot.com/2014/09/real-meditation-for-real-alcoholics.html
105 http://theconsciouslife.com/how-to-meditate-a-guide-for-beginners.htm

spirits." (p 152 *Alcoholic's Anonymous*) You can't really talk a person out of their fears and pat their hand to make the dread go way. Anyone who is trying to help the newcomer has to set an example and teach them ways to discipline their thoughts which in turn helps with their emotions. Many people in recovery meditate upon awakening and read one of several popular 12 Step meditation books But the more ritualistic forms of meditation work best to help a person find serenity. Always let them chose their own method of meditation so that they will more likely follow through when you are not there.

Presenting Problem NINE: Nervousness, General Anxiety, Stress

Although this is closely related to Presenting Problem Eight, *Fear, Panic Dread*, these symptoms are more a direct result of what the physical body is doing, as opposed to the emotional, in trying to regain balance internally. Just the fact that the system is throwing off poisons and trying to get the brain chemistry back in order is enough to deeply tax the nerves. Think of the "shakes" a person has coming off booze or the feeling of beetles crawling on the skin from the meth head. The body is under a great deal of stress and it shows itself as general anxiety in the detoxing person.

Factoid:[106] *According to a recent study, children who were exposed to methamphetamine in the womb may be at greater risk for behavior problems — including anxiety, depression, and moodiness.*

Good nutrition and supplements can really help. Of course I have already mentioned what Dr. Larry had us do at the Hand of Hope, which is to use calcium and magnesium to relax muscles and ease cramping. But there are other things you can do to help the body such as exercising, rock climbing, walking, steam baths, etc. Every little thing helps when coming off mind-affecting chemicals.

However, there are times when anxiety grows acute--a sort of mini panic attack. Often it is because the person under stress forgets to breathe properly. I know it sounds implausible, but

---
106 http://psychcentral.com/news/2012/03/21/meth-babies-at-greater-risk-for-anxiety-and-depression/36299.html

the exercise below may convince you this is so. The good thing is, we have another no-cost low-tech way to deal with anxiety and panic.

TRY THIS: Brain Breathing

From *Build Your Brain Power*[107] by Arthur Winter and Ruth Winter

During times of great mental stress and physical recuperation, less oxygen is taken into the body. This is because breathing patterns are interfered with under extreme stress.

Factoid:[108] *Our breath is an indicator of our mood and our mood is an indicator of our breath. This means that if we change how we breathe we can change our mood. It also means that when our mood changes so does our breath*

Snap your fingers about once a second.

---
107 https://amzn.to/2ZrH2VE
108 http://www.gaiamtv.com/article/10-interesting-facts-about-breathing

Exercise: Stand up and sit down. Do it *now* and then continue with this exercise. Snap your fingers about once a second. With each snap, shift your eyes to the right and the next snap to the left. Repeat 20 times.

OK. You are on the honor system that you did it. What happened to your breath pattern? You most likely didn't pay attention to the breath and your breathing became shallow in your chest? This type of respiration is inefficient and tension-producing. Your prospect is experiencing this much of the time in the first 30 days.

Reduced oxygen[109] levels have been shown to cause a decline in the neurotransmitter chemicals
   Dopamine
   Nor-epinephrine
   Serotonin

Improving the intake of oxygen efficiency may promote physical changes in the brain and improve the function.

Brain breathing exercises to teach those in early recovery:

1. Brain Breathing Deluxe

While standing, bend slightly forward and rest your palms on your knees. Let all the air out of your lungs through your mouth in shorts bursts while simultaneously sucking up your tummy. Flex your tummy in and out while all the air is out. Do it 3 or 4 times. Then breathe in through your nose filling up your lungs. Force your tummy in and out with full lungs. Then repeat the process 3 times.

2. Modified Brain Breathing

While standing or sitting, curl your lips over your teeth, leaving just a slit of your mouth open. Inhale deeply

---

109 **https://tinyurl.com/yyxfcohx**

through your nose. Exhale forcefully through the slit between your lips in a series of short, distinct bursts of air. After completely exhaling, take several relaxed breaths and repeat once or twice more.

Both these exercises will calm a person down and make them less anxious almost immediately.

Factoid:[110] *Breathing is essential to our survival and to our good health. We can live more than 50 days without food and about 7 days without water. But, without oxygen we cannot survive more than about 5 minutes. In many cultures, breath (qi, chi, prana) is considered the vital link to energy, awareness, composure, and ultimately to transcendence.*

RECAP

Proper breathing and air to the brain are important functions in maintaining physical and emotional health. The bottom line is that we must get enough oxygen to our brain and other organs for them to do the jobs they were intended to do. In times of stress, people actually forget to breathe! They are so focused on problems or their aggravation that they can go way too long without a good breath of air. The body reacts with panic and anxiety when it is deprived of the nourishment it needs. We can help newcomers when we teach them how to calm down by getting a burst of oxygen during stress.

---

110 https://sites.google.com/site/stanleyguansite/health/health-tips/breathe-deeply-to-activate-vagus-nerve

Presenting Problem TEN: Hopelessness or Alienation

When the alcoholic and addict lose hope and/or feels completely alienated, they become good candidates for giving up which leads to picking up. It might even lead to suicide. Back in the day, the old timers used to warn us not to dwell too much on our feelings. At least the negative ones. They didn't want us sitting on the pity pot, constantly grovelling and apologizing, they didn't want us feeling alone, useless, hopeless. All those feelings would lead us right back to the bottle and our drug of choice. But detoxing is a crazy time-- when our bodies are screaming for more of our chemicals and we have entirely too much time on our hands which may be devoted to thinking about ourselves and our troubles.

They told us there was nothing better for staying off booze than to work with another person that is still suffering from alcoholism (and today we include drug addiction). Bill Wilson, the co-founder of AA said it quite nicely in his story in the book of *Alcoholics Anonymous*.

> *My friend had emphasized the absolute necessity of demonstrating these principles in all my affairs. Particularly was it imperative to work with others as he had worked with me. Faith without works was dead, he said. And how appallingly true for the alcoholic! For if an alcoholic failed to perfect and enlarge his spiritual life through work and self-sacrifice for others, he could not survive the certain trials and low spots ahead. If he did not work, he would surely drink again, and if he drank, he would surely die. Then faith would be dead indeed. With us it is just like that.*

One of the first drafts for the original Big Book Cover of Alcoholics Anonymous First Edition" It Shows the intent of the publisher that it features the book as a "Pathway to a Cure." Dick B.s web site[111]

There wasn't much research on kindness back in the 1930's. Those early recovering drunks just knew it worked. Today we have lots of studies that tell us what the old timers discovered on their own. These studies have shown that the act of kindness has a positive effect on the immune system and it increases production of serotonin in the brain. "Serotonin is a naturally occurring neurochemical that has a calming, mood regulating, and anti-anxiety effect ... and it's regarded as a

---

111 http://www.drbob.info/photos.shtml

"feel good" substance because it serves as a pathway for pleasure in the brain." ~The Underground Health Reporter[112]

Again, back in the day... as soon as you had a day or two off booze, you were expected to start going on 12 Step calls under the guidance of your sponsor. Working with others that have the same infliction as you is powerful. So powerful is service that it has become the cornerstone of recovery. In fact, you reading this book is powerful. You want to help, find *better ways* to help, those who others have given up on or the ones too stubborn to agree to treatment. Your willingness to help is the energy that saves lives--no, I am not talking about saving *their life*--but yours!

Consequently, if you can get your prospect to somehow think of others, rather than wallow in his or her own troubles, you can get them to begin saving their own life. However, in the first few months and for a myriad of reasons, you may not want them traipsing down to the local detox ward and preaching to the inmates! You likely could not convince them this was a good idea anyway. So you must approach it creatively.

TRY THIS: Random Acts of Kindness

I recall the old timers telling us young'ens that to be spiritual we must do something really nice for someone and not tell anyone who did the good deed. Boy was that difficult! I wanted to do nice things for others and I *wanted* to tell on myself. But I didn't. Even now I could give you an example from my life, but feel it would jinx me. I can just hear my first sponsor, "Shelly, if you tell someone you did it, then you defeat your purpose in doing it." Even today I continue with this spiritual exercise. Sometimes it is a pay-it-forward type of

---

[112] http://undergroundhealthreporter.com/act-of-kindness/#ixzz3H7mksm7k

thing but most often it is a simple little anonymous kindness.

Factoid:[113] *Doing an act of kindness brings a sense of belonging and reduces isolation.*
Being a part of a social network leads to a feeling of belonging. Face-to-face activities such as volunteering at a drop-in center can help reduce loneliness and isolation.

In the first week or two, the newcomer is going to be too sick to think about doing random acts of kindness. But after a couple weeks, you may want to teach this behavior to your prospect. Start off with the exercise of doing one nice thing that day without telling anyone. If you are helping just one person, mark the days that they succeed but ask them not to tell you what they did! If you are working in a more formal setting, see how many can do it and how they feel about it. Discuss it in group. This is the beginning of service in a fun way-- yet it isn't too taxing and doesn't require great reserves of energy, knowledge and time, which they don't have right now.

Surprise that lonely lady down the street with a delivery of flowers from "a secret admirerer"

---

113 http://www.mentalhealth.org.uk/help-information/mental-health-a-z/A/altruisim/

As you explain this principle, differentiate kindness from other types of benevolence (shamelessly lifted from Trans4Mind):[114]

Kindness is based in an action.

Kindness is generally associated with small, non-essential gifts. (For example, if we give a lollipop to a child, that is "kindness"; in contrast, if we give $100 to a starving man, that might be called "charity.")

Kindness does not require reciprocity; (i.e., we do not expect anything in return--although we appreciate a "thank you" or a smile from the recipient of our kindness).

Kindness is not a favor (when we "do a favor," we expect that the other person would do a favor for us in the future.)

Kindness is an act of anonymity. It is "hit and run" (Sometimes we commit acts of kindness for people whom we do not meet. Even when our identity is known by the recipient, we do not linger to accept acclaim beyond the person's smile or a word of gratitude.)

Kindness is generally a spontaneous act. We see a need, and we fulfill it immediately.

Pay for the coffee of the guy behind you.

---

114 http://www.trans4mind.com/jamesharveystout/kindness.htm

Unless you are co-dependent, you won't have a whole lot of experience in thinking of others first. So it might be a good idea to explore these websites with your helpee and get some great ideas:

> SpreadKindness.org
> spreadkindness.org/tools/ideas
> Pay it Forward
> payitforwardday.com/
> 50 Acts of Kindness
> //thehalfwaypoint.net/2009/09/50-simple-ways-to-pay-it-forward/
> Facebook (if they are signed up)
> facebook.com/PF2014
> We make a living by what we get   (You should enjoy watching this together)
> facebook.com/video.php?v=657952077606425

We make a living by what we get.
We make a life by what we give.
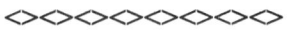

RECAP

Service to others is spirituality in action. Thinking of others and getting the focus off of self is one of the best ways to begin feeling good about yourself again. Studies show us that not only doing kind deeds but seeing someone else do kind deeds releases endorphins in our brain making us feel better. You are not a counselor, so its best not to "analyze" your helpee to figure out their problems--but teach them new behaviors. They can analyze themselves if needed. Random acts of kindness spark feelings of unity, usefulness, and spirituality.

And strangely, teaching kindness is truly one of the lowest cost of the low-tech strategies you can do for the person you help. This is the beginning of service work and puts them in a better space instantaneously.

Presenting Problem ELEVEN: General feelings of nausea, sickness, deep muscle pain, stress, nervousness

I travel to Alaska every summer and help my brother with his campground in the interior. I also carry my writing business with me, so when invited to go to an Athabaskan Fish Camp that also served as a drug and alcohol treatment center for locals, I jumped at the chance to write an article about it. I hitched a ride with a couple young men who were going there for drug treatment. It took hours and hours under the hot sun to navigate the Tanana River and tributaries before we arrived in the late afternoon. Then abruptly our transportation slipped away leaving us trapped with the mosquitoes in a remote fish camp--no running water, hotels, phones, TVs, radios, or roads to leave by. This was truly bush country.

However, a unique opportunity awaited me. I experienced how treatment, the native way, works. It has long been said that American Indian populations have difficulty with the western European method of recovery--they needed (and need) something more oriented to their culture. What they did at this camp for treatment was work the guys hard during the day, then sit in a sweat lodge each evening and then finished the day telling their stories (like an AA meeting) around a campfire. The leader was an elder Athabaskan with 16 years sobriety using a combination of Native inspired recovery and AA principles.

What impressed me the most was just how fast they got fit physically. By the end of the first week these young men were in great shape while in our Minnesota Model Treatment Centers, detox was a lot more complicated physically. Now don't think these men weren't in bad shape when they arrived--they were very very sick. Thinking about it--I was sure that the sweat lodge that extracted poisons from the body was a form of rapid detox.

Factoid:[115] *Most cultures around the world have their own versions of the sweat bath, whether it's the ancient Romans and their "Thermae" or the traditional Japanese "Onsen". The Russians call it the "Banya" and the for native North American Indians it's "Inipi", without omitting the notorious Turkish bath or "Hamam". However, the most prominent and popular one of all is the Finnish Sauna.*

Although after the 2010 Sweat Lodge tragedy in Arizona[116] where 3 people died, some experts claimed that you aren't supposed to try and detox the body at all, it is a process the body does on its own. That is foolishness. People have been helping the body detox since we came out of the caves and found natural hot springs. In fact, the skin and sweating is one of the main methods the body uses to clean itself.

Skin is the largest organ[117] of the body and one of its main functions is removing impurities from within. Detoxification is the opposite if intoxication and helping the skin do its job can facilitate a safe detox. What happened in Arizona was unsafe. The lodge was too hot, the participants did not replenish water and nutrients dehydrating from their bodies, and their "guru" way overdid everything including his belief in his own expertise. Some paid the ultimate price.

This is another good example of why I say, "Remember, you

---
115 http://www.pureinsideout.com/benefits-of-sauna.html
116 https://tinyurl.com/y3qxtp99
117 https://tinyurl.com/y3ulsjfh

are not their doctor, pastor, or guru. You are a friend helping them get off alcohol and drugs. They make their own decisions and you only guide them--seeing that all the information they need to make informed decisions is available.

TRY THIS: Give Them the Sobriety Spa Treatment

SOBRIETY SPA TREATMENT ONE: Put them in Hot Water

Drugs are poisons to the body. We say DETOX because we are detoxing them from various poisons that interfere with bodily functions, mental functions, and moods, causing a slow erosion of what makes us ourselves. Poisonous deposits are stored in the cells, fat, and organs of the body.

They need to come out as quickly as possible. As long as the toxins remain in the body--traces of them can re-stimulate or "trigger" cravings, pain, confusion, and fear.

Any type of regulated heat that produces a sweat works. Cultures in Europe, Asia and many island peoples understand how important hot water is to our health. Other than hot tubs at hotel and gyms, medical professionals in the U.S. are a bit behind the rest of the world. For heavens sake, the Native Americans in the U.S. know how valuable hot water is to healing. The sanitariums (vacation, spa, health resorts) all have steam rooms and hot tubs to help people detox and relax. A number of treatment centers on the islands use these same methods. Hot water, steam, and radiant heat are not just for spoiled pampered women to feel luxurious; it is a healing mechanism.

"The research shows our ancestors got it right. It makes you feel better. It makes the joints looser. It reduces pain and it seems to have a somewhat prolonged effect that goes beyond the period of immersion," says Bruce E. Becker, MD, director of the National Aquatics & Sports Medicine Institute at Washington State University in Spokane. ~ArthritisToday.org

Here are some hot water healing methods to incorporate into the recovery plan:

Hot Tubs
Saunas (Scandanavian)
Parnaiya or Banya (Russian)
Sweat Lodges (Native Americans)
Steam Rooms
Herbal Wraps
Hot Bathes with Epson salts
Foot Soaks (a favorite of Canyon Ranches)[118]

◇◇◇◇◇◇◇◇

Factoid:[119] *Coconut water is from young, green coconuts and is low in calories and a natural source of electrolytes including sodium and potassium. Eight ounces of coconut water has 46 calories, 9 grams of carbohydrates, 250 mg of sodium, 600 mg of potassium, 60 mg of magnesium, 45 mg of phosphorus, and 2 grams of protein.*

◇◇◇◇◇◇◇◇

---

118 https://tinyurl.com/y3nvhvbh
119 https://tinyurl.com/n62uztw

Precautions:

a) Really hot water (anything over 100°) is contraindicated for those with heart conditions, pregnancies, certain skin conditions--so always check with their primary health care professional before using water over 100°

b) Have them *drink* plenty of water too and keep their electrolytes up. Not following this is one reason those people died in Arizona. A lot of folks like sports drinks for this, but I prefer to drink coconut water. You can also use a pinch of sea salt in your water to keep hydrated.

c) If your charge is really sick and out of it in the first days, you might not want them in a tub of water alone where they could have a seizure or drop off to sleep. Begin using hot water by giving them a foot soak once a day. Be sure to add 1/2 cup of Epson salts to a container of water. Epsom salt helps flush toxins and heavy metals from your skin, increase circulation and ease muscle cramps and joint pain.

And as an added benefit, it is very hard to be pissed off and cranky when sitting in a tub of hot water.

SOBRIETY SPA TREATMENT TWO   Give Them Massages

Massage is the intentional handling of the body's soft tissues for therapeutic effect. Touch heals on so many levels, the body, the mind, the moods, the spirit. Advantages of massage are so numerous volumes have been written about it. The University of Minnesota Wellness website[120] lists a myriad of benefits from massage is including such diverse things as:

---

120 https://tinyurl.com/bu9oweu

Physical relaxation
Improved circulation, which nourishes cells and improves waste elimination
Relief for tight muscles (knots) and other aches and pains
Release of nerve compression (carpel tunnel, sciatica)
Greater flexibility and range of motion
Enhanced energy and vitality
Decreases pain and increases functioning in these conditions:
Carpal tunnel syndrome
Sciatica
Tension headaches
Whiplash
Tendon and muscle tears
Varicose veins
Back pain
Sore or overused muscles (prevents and treats)
Gout
Rheumatoid arthritis
Osteoarthritis
Diabetes
Hypertension
Reduces risk of chronic diseases, such as heart disease, diabetes, autoimmune diseases
Improved mood
Reduced anxiety
Lower stress levels
Lessening of depression
Reduced anger and aggression
Improved sleep patterns and decreased sleep disturbance
Reduced fatigue
Enhances immune system
Improves athletic performance and enhances recovery

Massage Myth:[121] Massage Can Get Rid of Cellulite. This is a favorite treatment in some spas and salons. Cellulite is FAT and it would be very nice to think that we could get rid of our fat by having a massage! However, there are only four ways to get rid of fat: exercising, eating less, surgery, and cryogenics.

Fortunately messages are relatively easy to get and are low cost too, depending on how you do it. In almost every area of the country, masseuses are available to come right to your door for around $100. If you are a small facility using this book, consider contracting with a licensed masseuse and incorporate it as part of the physical therapy. If you don't have funds for this, think about trading space for weekly massages for your clients.

You can also have clients massage each other (men with men and women with women). This way you are introducing them to service work (making another feel good) and they receive the benefit of touch. It is best to have them stick to head, neck, and massaging hands.

You can also teach clients to massage themselves--the foot massage, reflexology, is a good place to start--especially just after the hot foot soak mentioned above.

If you are the home helper and neither of you has the funds for things like massages--well, give them a neck rub or hand massage with a sweet smelling oil and when they are well enough, they might reciprocate.

Not only are are there numerous health benefits but it just

---

121 https://tinyurl.com/yycmoftu

makes you feel special and pampered--something in short supply with the alcoholic and addict. Touch is important in feeling connected (like hugs in meetings). We all need to be touched whether we know it or not.

Precautions.

a) Get males for the men and females for the women and don't allow naked massages--underwear or bathing suits required.

b) If you get clients to massage each other, be sure to limit it to the head, neck, hands and feet and use same sex partners.

c) Don't allow clients to experiment on each other when the therapy might be dangerous (walking on the back) or the volunteer has health problems that preclude even simple touching like skin diseases or multiple bruises.

RECAP

There are numerous advantages in teaching good habits so that the newcomer learns to destress, detox, relieve tension, calm nerves, and get a good night's sleep. In addition to prayer and meditation, we can concentrate on the body through healing hot water and healing touch. Many centers, such as Crossroads of Antigua,[122] understand how difficult it is to detox from drugs and alcohol and they understand that hot water therapies and massage speed up the body's natural healing processes. The benefits are numerous and cost can be kept low making these methods practical for home assisted detox, low cost clinic alternatives, and early recovery.

---

[122] http://crossroadsantigua.org/complementary_therapies/

Presenting Problem TWELVE: Rough time sleeping and/or drowsiness even after full night's sleep

Do not get angry or frustrated with your prospect if he or she is sleepy during the day and has insomnia at night. The inability to sleep[123] is one of the outer symptoms when the brain is trying to repair itself. You should expect to see it in the newly recovering. The old timers didn't want us taking sleeping pills and so told us, "Stop whining, no one ever died from lack of sleep!" And so many a newcomer went around in a half sleepy fog for months before they got into more regular sleep patterns.

This is one case where we don't need to be stuck in the past. There is evidence-based methods to deal with sleeplessness without taking mind-affecting chemicals. We already talked about eating that potato just before bed. You can also use the other calming and stress relieving techniques we covered such as meditation, hot water, and massage just before bed. Mom's tried and true cup of hot chocolate before bed has more truth that you knew. Turns out warm milk contains tryptophan,

---

123 https://tinyurl.com/y4vnfmlh

which is an amino acid that helps induce sleep. Turkey also contain tryptophan. That is one reason, besides overeating, that people get so sleepy after a big Thanksgiving dinner.

Some centers don't want to give hot chocolate because of the sugar but in the early recovery stage we probably need a bit of sugar anyway. There is however one potent and scientifically supported natural way to help induce sleep.

TRY THIS: Ask if they want Melatonin 1 Hour before Bed

Melatonin is a hormone produced in the pineal gland and is secreted at night or in the dark regulating sleep. Melatonin peaks in the body around 2 am and decreases until the next night and its time to sleep again. People who fly on jets use it to regulate sleep when flying across continents through time zones where the sleep cycle is disrupted.

After age 40, the body's production of melatonin diminishes with each year. You may have had a grandparent who went to bed at 7 pm, woke up at 3 am and then dozed off throughout the day. This is generally attributed to the lack of melatonin in their body. Even though they sleep all night--they don't sleep deeply enough to get restorative rest. Then they nap throughout the day. This is what it is like for the newly recovering--their whole system is distraught and taxed and not working well. Sleep is a big problem and melatonin may help.

There are a few contraindications for taking this hormone such as those who suffer from migraines and/or take the class of drugs called serotonin reuptakes (including but not limited to Celexa, Lexapro, Cipralex, Prozac, Luvox, Pacil, and Seroxat). These are drugs for depression, overeating, panic attacks, anxiety disorders and such. If they are taking medications for any of these or suffer from migraine headaches, melatonin can increase or cause headaches and is not recommended. (Stick to the potato.)

For the most part, research shows that side effects[124] of taking this supplement are minimal to none and the dosage doesn't have to be large. The dosage works well at 1 mg. (Some people take up to 5 mg a night but in double blind studies 1 mg worked just as well.)

Notice that the title of this last section is "Ask if they want Melatonin 1 Hour before Bed" not "Give them Melatonin 1 Hour before Bed." You are not to *give medications or supplements* unless you are under the supervision of a professional. This would be the physician who is supervising the detox or a professional from a home assisted clinic. So you provide support and information and they make the decision about which of these low-cost low tech approaches they want to use in the first 30 to 90 days of abstinence.

My life is a good example of how this works. It was years ago after turning 40 that I began taking melatonin and shared my success with my brother. I travel extensively and afternoons on the road had been a real challenge for me. I often had to pull over while traveling in a car and catch a snooze. I called this my three o'clock slump. Almost from the first day of taking melatonin I noticed that I no longer got so sleepy-eyed at three in the afternoon. My night time sleep was deeper with less interruption and real rest--like in my younger years.

Initially skeptical, my brother was also beginning to feel his age and decided to try melatonin. A month later he phoned, "Shelly, melatonin has saved my life." I have since suggested this to many people and except for a few, those who chose to take it noticed much improvement in their lives--the kinds of improvement that come from getting a good night's sleep.

---

124 https://tinyurl.com/y3q9wpjj

RECAP

We know that alcoholics in withdrawal suffer from sleep disorders and often they are the direct result of melatonin issues along with circadian disturbances.[125] We also know that alcohol itself has a *direct* "inhibitory effect on pineal melatonin synthesis."[126] If we can do such a simple thing as get our helpee a solid good nights sleep, we will be doing them a huge favor in putting them on solid ground for healing their battered body.

---

125 http://www.ncbi.nlm.nih.gov/pubmed/19029096
126 http://www.ncbi.nlm.nih.gov/pubmed/8888105

3. Final Thoughts

The point of this book is to help those that are trying to help alcoholics and addicts get off their drugs when regular treatment either can't or won't be used. Although far from a medical manual, read disclaimer again, there are many low cost, low tech methods that are highly effective during the first few months of recovery. This manual is designed to counter the "tomato effect" in medicine.

The "tomato effect" was coined by Goodwin and Goodwin (1984) in the Journal of the American Medical Association,[127] where they contrasted this to the well known "placebo effect" where a treatment that seemed to work was later shown to be useless and possibly harmful. The tomato effect is the opposite whereby medical professionals reject highly efficacious therapies because they are not the party line so to speak.

Factoid:[128] *The word placebo comes from the Latin phrase, "I shall please," future indicative of placere "to please." Medical sense is first recorded 1785, "a medicine given more to please than to benefit the patient."*

The story of the tomato was that people in the new world thought it was poisonous and refused to have anything to do with it while a farmer by the name of Robert G. Johnson from Salem, N.J. made headlines in 1820 by sitting on the Salem courthouse steps and eating a tomato in plain sight. He did this day after day and survived to the amazement of all. Because of his tenacity, he convinced farmers to begin

---

127 http://jama.jamanetwork.com/article.aspx?articleid=392749
128 http://www.etymonline.com/index.php?term=placebo

growing this nutritious crop and the tomato slowly became a popular North American edible. Over the last 80 years of the 20th century, the tomato has become the largest commercial crop in the United States.

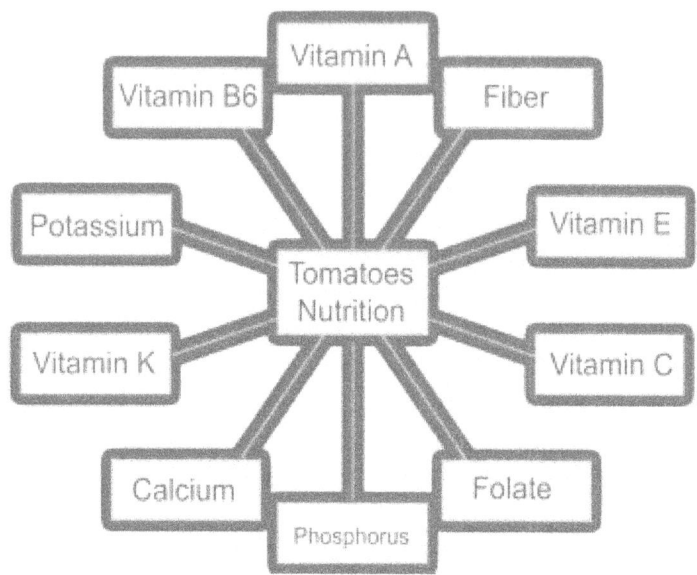

The experts called this fruit "poisonous"

Factoid:[129] *THE TOMATO (Lycopersicon esculentum) is a New World plant, originally found in Peru and carried back to Spain from whence it quickly spread to Italy (pommidoro) and France, where it was known as the pomme d'amour and thought to have aphrodisiac properties. By 1560, the tomato was becoming a staple of the continental European diet.*

The Old-timers in the 12 Step programs learned by trial and error that some things worked better than others with alcoholics and addicts. Since the thirties, researchers and

---

129 http://jama.jamanetwork.com/article.aspx?articleid=392749

others have added to this body of knowledge. People have been intoxicating themselves and then detoxifying themselves for millennia. And recovery need not be complicated and expensive, although it can be.

This manual helps bring the wisdom of the old timers combined with evidence based solutions so that you can help the alcoholic and addict leave their dependencies behind and get back into life.

The main thing to remember is that you do not want to take responsibility for the medical aspects of their detox because it can be life threatening. Please rely on professionals for the physical withdrawal during the first few months. In addition you are not their psychiatrist--you can make information available and make suggestions but it works best if you let your helpee choose their own own approaches to recovery. That is not to say you don't try to funnel them toward healthy choices and keep a reign on some of the information available to them...but that is up to you.

Ultimately the decisions are up to the person you are working with. Thank you for joining us in the fantastic role of being of service to others. It is often a thankless job, but the rewards for you will be great. It is an exercise in spiritual development and as they say in AA, "surely you will meet some of us as you trudge the road of happy destiny."

About Day By Day Recovery Resources

Day By Day is a small grass roots publishing house that continues the work of those that brought you the classic Day By Day[130] (published by Hazelden). We don't publish many titles but the ones we publish, people in recovery *do* read. In fact, they read our titles with more interest and focus than most other recovery books. Why? Because the content comes from others in recovery. We record and repeat what those in recovery from alcoholism and addiction tell us in meetings, in person, in writing. We've collected the wisdom of recovery from the Old-timers and put it together so you have instant access. It makes sense. We don't get complicated. We keep it simple and we tell you the truth. All our grassroots recovery books are sold at our Amazon.com/daybyday[131] store as well as our online store at PocketSponsor.com/storefront.html[132]

World's Smallest Recovery Meditation Book (2 inches by 3 inches) FREE

---

130 http://www.day-by-day.org/
131 https://www.amazon.com/daybyday
132 http://www.pocketsponsor.com/storefront.html

If you like this text, then you will also like the *Pocket Sponsor Thumbnail* for helping newcomers. This is the world's smallest recovery meditation book. It is so small it will fit in your wallet or shirt pocket. We'll send you a free copy if you go to the website and fill out the online form. (no strings attached) PocketSponsor.com/freethumbnail.html

Deepest Discounts in the Industry (up to 40%)

We offer deep discounts, **up to 40%**, to groups and organizations. We can offer you these kind of discounts because we keep our overhead low—no storefront—and most of our advertising is customer referral. So please tell your groups, sober friends, treatment centers, and other organizations about our motivating titles and how low our prices are.

Here is a list of the more popular books that we carry.

$9 **PocketSponsor.com** (24/7 Back to the Basics support for addiction recovery) *BUY NOW from Amazon https://amzn.to/2GVbelK*

$12 **SittinginPictures.org** (Vision Meditations, a Hopi tradition for healing) *BUY NOW from Amazon https://amzn.to/2Koietn*

$6.95 **Color Me Sober** (31 day coloring journal based on the 12 Step slogans) *BUY NOW from Amazon https://amzn.to/31xP1Ch*

$14 **YoungSoberFree.com** (by and for Young Adults in Recovery) *BUY NOW from Amazon https://amzn.to/2YQcQaC*

$12.95 **WalkSoftlyandCarryABigBook.com** (Sloganeering—Digital & Paperback) *BUY NOW from Amazon https://amzn.to/2KlYnuU*

$12.95 **RespectMeRules.com** *(Stop Verbal and Emotional Abuse in its Tracks)* ***BUY NOW*** *from Amazon https://amzn.to/2YCsU0r*

The circle stands for the whole world of A.A., and the triangle stands for A.A.'s Three Legacies: Recovery, Unity, and Service. Within our wonderful new world, we have found freedom from our fatal obsession. ~*Alcoholics Anonymous Comes of Age* (p. 139), Bill W.'s 1955 speech

In 1994 the AA General Service Conference decided to discontinue using the circle and triangle logo on all Conference-approved literature. Today, however, it is still associated with many types of 12-Step programs. The symbol continues to have a special meaning for people all over the world in recovery from mind affecting chemicals.

www.ingramcontent.com/pod-product-compliance
Lightning Source LLC
Chambersburg PA
CBHW070643050426
42451CB00008B/289